Math Contests
for
High School
Volume 3

School Years: 1991-92 through 1995-96

Written by

Steven R. Conrad • Daniel Flegler

Published by MATH LEAGUE PRESS
Printed in the United States of America

Cover art by Bob DeRosa

Phil Frank Cartoons Copyright © 1993 by CMS

First Printing, 1996
Copyright © 1996
by Mathematics Leagues Inc.
All Rights Reserved

No part of this publication may be reproduced or trans-
mitted in any form or by any means, electronic or mech-
anical, including photocopy, recording, or any information
storage or retrieval system, or any other means, without
written permission from the publisher. Requests for permission or further information should be addressed to:

Math League Press
P.O. Box 720
Tenafly, NJ 07670-0720

ISBN 0-940805-11-1

Preface

Math Contests—High School, Volume 3 is the third volume in our series of problem books for high school students. The first two volumes contain contests given in the school years 1979-80 through 1990-91. Volume 3 contains contests given from 1991-92 through 1995-96. (Use the order form on page 70 to order any of our 9 books.)

These books gives classes, clubs, teams, and individuals diversified collections of high school math problems. All of these contests were used in regional interscholastic competition throughout the United States and Canada. Each contest was taken by about 80 000 students. In the contest section, each page contains a complete contest that can be worked during a 30-minute period. The convenient format makes this book easy to use in a class, a math club, or for just plain fun. In addition, detailed solutions for each contest also appear on a single page.

Every contest has questions from different areas of mathematics. The goal is to encourage interest in mathematics through solving *worthwhile* problems. Many students first develop an interest in mathematics through problem-solving activities such as these contests. On each contest, the last two questions are generally more difficult than the first four. The final question on each contest is intended to challenge the very best mathematics students. The problems require no knowledge beyond secondary school mathematics. No knowledge of calculus is required to solve any of these problems. From two to four questions on each contest are accessible to students with only a knowledge of elementary algebra. Starting with the 1992-93 school year, students have been permitted to use any calculator on any of our contests.

This book is divided into four sections for ease of use by both students and teachers. The first section of the book contains the contests. Each contest contains six questions that can be worked in a 30-minute period. The second section of the book contains detailed solutions to all the contests. Often, several solutions are given for a problem. Where appropriate, notes about interesting aspects of a problem are mentioned on the solutions page. The third section of the book consists of a listing of the answers to each contest question. The last section of the book contains the difficulty rating percentages for each question. These percentages (based on actual student performance on these contests) determine the relative difficulty of each question.

You may prefer to consult the answer section rather than the solution section when first reviewing a contest. The authors believe that reworking a problem when the answer (but *not* the solution) is known often helps to better understand problem-solving techniques.

Revisions have been made to the wording of some problems for the sake of clarity and correctness. The authors welcome comments you may have about either the questions or the solutions. Though we believe there are no errors in this book, each of us agrees to blame the other should any errors be found!

Steven R. Conrad & Daniel Flegler, contest authors

Acknowledgments

For the beauty, cleverness, and breadth of his numerous mathematical contributions, we are indebted to Michael Selby.

For her continued patience and understanding, special thanks to Marina Conrad, whose only mathematical skill, an important one, is the ability to count the ways.

For her lifetime support and encouragement, special thanks to Mildred Flegler.

To Daniel Will-Harris, whose skill in graphic design is exceeded only by his skill in writing *really* funny computer books, thanks for help when we needed it most: the year we first began to typeset these contests on a computer.

Table Of Contents

The Contests

November, 1991 – April, 1996

Contest Number 1   October 29, 1991

Name _____ **Teacher** _____ **Grade Level** _____ **Score** _____

Time Limit: 30 minutes   *Answer Column*

1-1.	What are all real values of x which satisfy $\sqrt{1 \times 9 \times 9 \times 1} = x^2$?	1-1.
1-2.	What is the positive integer N for which $N + 2N + 3N + 4N = 10^N$?	1-2.
1-3.	In a circle, a certain chord is the perpendicular bisector of a radius, as shown. If the length of this chord is $6\sqrt{3}$, what is the area of this circle?	1-3.
1-4.	There is only one set of four consecutive positive integers such that the sum of the cubes of three of them is equal to the cube of the remaining one. What is the smallest of these four integers?	1-4.
1-5.	What are all real values of $x > 1$ for which $\frac{6}{x}$ is an integer?	1-5.
1-6.	What are all real values of x for which $|x^2 - 4| - 3x \le 0$?	1-6.

© 1991 by Mathematics Leagues Inc.

HIGH SCHOOL MATHEMATICS CONTESTS

Math League Press, P.O. Box 720, Tenafly, New Jersey 07670-0720

Contest Number 2   **December 3, 1991**

Name _____ Teacher _____ Grade Level ____ Score ____

Time Limit: 30 minutes   *Answer Column*

2-1. Find *any one* ordered 4-tuple of positive integers (a,b,c,d) for which $a + b + c + d = 20$ and $abcd = 81$.

2-1.

2-2. The sum of the lengths of the two legs of a right triangle is 20. What is the smallest possible length of the hypotenuse of this triangle?

2-2.

2-3. If $x + 2x + 4x + 8x = k + \dfrac{k}{2} + \dfrac{k}{4} + \dfrac{k}{8}$, and $k \neq 0$, what is the ratio of x to k?

2-3.

2-4. If $3x - 3y + z - w = 7$ and $5x - y + 3z + w = 3$, what is the value of $x + y + z + w$?

2-4.

2-5. What are the three ordered pairs of numbers (x,y) for which the four vertices of a parellelogram are $(0,0)$, $(3,0)$, and $(4,4)$, and (x,y)?

2-5.

2-6. The solution of the inequality

$$\frac{1}{x - 1} + \frac{1}{x - 2} + \frac{1}{x - 3} \geq 1$$

is the union of a finite number of disjoint intervals, each of the form $a < x \leq b$. If the *length* of the interval $a < x \leq b$ is defined as $b - a$, what is the sum of the lengths of all these intervals?

2-6.

© 1991 by Mathematics Leagues Inc.

Solutions on Page 35 • Answers on Page 66   3

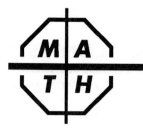

HIGH SCHOOL MATHEMATICS CONTESTS

Math League Press, P.O. Box 720, Tenafly, New Jersey 07670-0720

Contest Number 3 | **January 7, 1992**

Name _____ Teacher _____ Grade Level ____ Score ____

Time Limit: 30 minutes | *Answer Column*

3-1. The sum of 1991 positive integers is 1992. What is the value of the largest one of these integers? | 3-1.

3-2. What is the positive value of x which satisfies $3^{-2} + 4^{-2} = x^{-2}$? | 3-2.

3-3. The coordinates of the vertices of a triangle are $(0,0)$, $(a,0)$, and $(0,b)$, where a and b are both integers. If the area of this triangle is 1, what are all possible values of a? | 3-3.

3-4. Although there is no positive integer a for which $36a + 1$ is equal to $3a^2$, for what positive integer a is the value of $36a + 1$ most nearly equal to the value of $3a^2$? | 3-4.

3-5. A fourth degree polynomial P has integer coefficients, and its leading coefficient is 1. If $P(\sqrt{2} + \sqrt{7}) = 0$, what is the value of $P(1)$? | 3-5.

3-6. In the diagram of $\triangle ABC$ shown at the right, $\overline{AE}$, $\overline{BF}$, and $\overline{CD}$ intersect at point P. If the area of $\triangle AFP$ is 40, the area of $\triangle CFP$ is 30, and the area of $\triangle CEP$ is 35, what is the area of $\triangle BPD$? | 3-6.

© 1992 by Mathematics Leagues Inc.

4   Solutions on Page 36 • Answers on Page 66

Contest Number 4   **February 7, 1978**

Name _____ Teacher _____ Grade Level _____ Score ____

Time Limit: 30 minutes   *Answer Column*

4-1.   What are all integers n for which $1^n + 2^n = 3^n$?   4-1.

4-2.   What is the volume of a rectangular solid whose faces have areas   4-2.
       6, 8, and 12?

4-3.   What are all values of x for which $x(x+1) = (1991)(1992)$?   4-3.

4-4.   From the table   4-4.

1	2	3	...	k	...	15
16	17	18	...	$15+k$	...	30
31	32	33	...	$30+k$	...	45
...	...	...	...	...	...	...
211	212	213	...	$210+k$	...	225

of the first 225 natural numbers, 15 numbers are chosen so that no
two lie in the same row or the same column. What is the largest
possible sum of these 15 numbers?

4-5.   A small circle is inscribed in a 60° sector of a large circle, so the   4-5.
       small circle is tangent to all 3 sides of the sector. What is the ratio
       of the area of the small circle to the area of the sector?

4-6.   What is the positive value of x which satisfies   4-6.

$$\sqrt{x^2 + x + 1} + \sqrt{x^2 - x + 1} = 4?$$

© 1992 by Mathematics Leagues Inc.

Solutions on Page 37 • Answers on Page 66

5

Contest Number 5   **March 3, 1992**

Name _____ Teacher _____ Grade Level _____ Score _____

Time Limit: 30 minutes   *Answer Column*

5-1.   If $x + y = 5$ and $x - y = 1$, what is the value of $2^{x^2 - y^2}$?   5-1.

5-2.   In a 30°-60°-90° triangle, the difference between the length of the longest side and the length of the shortest side is 1992. What is the length of the longest side?   5-2.

5-3.   Find the smallest positive number x for which $\tan^2 x + \sec^2 x = 1$. [NOTE: Be sure to express your answer in radians.].   5-3.

5-4.   If $x^{10} + x^5 = 2^{10} + 2^5$, what are all possible values of x^5?   5-4.

5-5.   The number 43210 *contains* the combination "32;" the numbers 43120 and 42310 do not contain the combination "32." How many 5-digit numbers (between 10000 and 100000) contain the combination "32"?   5-5.

5-6.   If the roots of the equation $x^2 - (a + 1)x + a + 4 = 0$ are negative, what are all possible values of the real number a?   5-6.

© 1992 by Mathematics Leagues Inc.

Contest Number 6   April 7, 1992

Name _____ Teacher _____ Grade Level ____ Score ____

Time Limit: 30 minutes	*Answer Column*
6-1. If $1991x + 1991y = 1992(x + y)$, and $xy \neq 0$, what is the value of $\frac{x}{y}$?	6-1.
6-2. On his birthday, Brian was 14 years old and his father was 41. Brian noticed that his age was the reverse of his father's age. How old will Brian be the next time his age is the reverse of his father's?	6-2.
6-3. In convex quadrilateral $ABCD$, $AB = AD = 10$, $CB = CD = 17$, and $BD = 16$. What is the area of quadrilateral $ABCD$?	6-3.
6-4. What is the smallest positive integer x for which $4^{100} < 8^x$?	6-4.
6-5. What are all values of x for which $\log_x 5 = \log_5 x$?	6-5.
6-6. If x is *not* the square of an integer, then the value of $$7 + \sqrt{x} + \frac{1}{5 - \sqrt{x}}$$ is a rational number for only one positive integer x. What is this value of x?	6-6.

© 1992 by Mathematics Leagues Inc.

HIGH SCHOOL MATHEMATICS CONTESTS

Math League Press, P.O. Box 720, Tenafly, New Jersey 07670-0720

Contest Number 1   *Any calculator is always allowed.* Answers must be exact *or* have 4 (or more) significant digits, correctly rounded.   **October 27, 1992**

Name _____ **Teacher** _____ **Grade Level** ____ **Score** ____

Time Limit: 30 minutes   *Answer Column*

1-1. Jack wrote 100 positive numbers between 0 and 3, but he did not write the number 1. Jill wrote the reciprocal of every one of Jack's numbers. How many of these 200 numbers were between 0 and 1?	1-1.
1-2. What is the only integer n for which $\sqrt{n}$, $\sqrt{n+1}$, and $\sqrt{n+2}$ are the lengths of the sides of a right triangle?	1-2.
1-3. How many equilateral triangles of side–length 1 are needed to completely cover the interior of an equilateral triangle of side–length 10?	1-3.
1-4. What is the only real number x which satisfies $\sqrt{1992} = 1992\sqrt{x}$?	1-4.
1-5. The World Series of baseball, a famous sporting event, is played between two teams. As soon as either team wins 4 games, that team is declared World Champions (no game can end in a tie). If a World Series is played between two teams of equal ability (so that each team's probability of winning any game is $\frac{1}{2}$), what is the probability that World Champions are declared after only 4 games?	1-5.
1-6. In a country whose currency consists of $6 bills and $11 bills, the price of every item sold is a whole number of dollars that can be paid *exactly*, without need for "change," using only these two types of bills. What is the largest whole number of dollars which could *not* be the price of an item sold in this country?	1-6.

© 1992 by Mathematics Leagues Inc.

Solutions on Page 40 • Answers on Page 66

HIGH SCHOOL MATHEMATICS CONTESTS

Math League Press, P.O. Box 720, Tenafly, New Jersey 07670-0720

Contest Number 2 *Any calculator is always allowed.* Answers must be exact *or* have 4 (or more) significant digits, correctly rounded. **December 1, 1992**

Name _____ Teacher _____ Grade Level _____ Score _____

Time Limit: 30 minutes | *Answer Column*

2-1. The number 9 can be written as the sum of 9 consecutive integers. What is the product of these 9 integers? | 2-1.

2-2. The sum of the two (linear) factors of $x^2 - 26x + 144$ is subtracted from the sum of the two (linear) factors of $x^2 - 25x + 144$. What is the value of the result? | 2-2.

2-3. If $x = -664$, determine, in simplest form, the value of
$$\Big|\,\big|\,|x| - x\,\big| - x\,\Big|.$$ | 2-3.

2-4. What are all values of x which satisfy $\dfrac{2x-1}{x+1} \le 1$? | 2-4.

2-5. What is the distance from the origin to the graph of
$$y = \sqrt{6x - x^2 - 9}\,?$$ | 2-5.

2-6. Two congruent semicircles lie on the diameter of a third semicircle, each tangent to the other two. A small circle is tangent to all three semicircles. If the area of the shaded region is 45π, what is the length of a radius of the small circle? | 2-6.

© 1992 by Mathematics Leagues Inc.

HIGH SCHOOL MATHEMATICS CONTESTS

Math League Press, P.O. Box 720, Tenafly, New Jersey 07670-0720

Contest Number 3   *Any calculator is always allowed.* Answers must be exact *or* have 4 (or more) significant digits, correctly rounded.   **January 5, 1993**

Name _____ Teacher _____ Grade Level _____ Score _____

Time Limit: 30 minutes   *Answer Column*

3-1.   What is the only integer n for which $\sqrt{n^2 + 1}$ is also an integer?   3-1.

3-2.   What are all values of x which satisfy $x(x^2 - 1993) = x(x^2 - x)$?   3-2.

3-3.   The lengths of the diagonals of a parallelogram are 10 and 24. If the length of one side of the parallelogram is 13, what is the perimeter of the parallelogram?   3-3.

3-4.   The entries in a 7×7 *magic square* array of numbers are the integers 1 through 49 inclusive. The sum of the entries in every row, in every column, and in both major diagonals is the same, and is called the "magic" sum. What is the value of this "magic" sum?   3-4.

3-5.   The statement

   "There are exactly 25 prime numbers less than n."

is true when $n = 100$. For how many positive integers n (other than 100) is the statement true?   3-5.

3-6.   Among all ordered pairs of real numbers (x,y) which satisfy

$$x^4 + y^4 = x^2 + y^2,$$

what is the largest value of x?   3-6.

© 1993 by Mathematics Leagues Inc.

   Solutions on Page 42 • Answers on Page 66

Contest Number 4 *Any calculator is always allowed.* Answers must be exact *or* have 4 (or more) significant digits, correctly rounded. **February 2, 1993**

Name _____ Teacher _____ Grade Level _____ Score _____

Time Limit: 30 minutes   *Answer Column*

4-1. If $2^{x-3} = 1$ and $5^{y+2} = 1$, what is the value of $2^x 5^y$?   4-1.

4-2. The product of 1993 consecutive integers is 0. What is the greatest possible value for the largest one of these integers?   4-2.

4-3. If N is a positive integer, and if N^{50} is a 16-digit number, what is the value of N?   4-3.

4-4. Find the area of the region bounded by the graphs of the equations   4-4.

$x = -2$, $y = 0$, $x = 3$, and $y = |x + 2| + |x - 3|$.

4-5. What is the perimeter of a right tri-angle with hypotenuse 65 which can be circumscribed about a circle with radius 12?   4-5.

4-6. Let [x] denote the *greatest integer* ≤ x. For example, [2.345] = 2. Let ⟨x⟩ denote the *fractional part* of x, so that [x] + ⟨x⟩ = x. For example, ⟨2.345⟩ = 0.345, and [2.345] + ⟨2.345⟩ = 2.345. Also, three positive numbers a, b, and c form a *geometric progression* if $\frac{a}{b} = \frac{b}{c}$.   4-6.

What is the only positive real number x for which ⟨x⟩, [x], and x form a geometric progression?

© 1993 by Mathematics Leagues Inc.

HIGH SCHOOL MATHEMATICS CONTESTS

Math League Press, P.O. Box 720, Tenafly, New Jersey 07670-0720

Contest Number 5   *Any calculator is always allowed.* Answers must be exact *or* have 4 (or more) significant digits, correctly rounded.   **March 2, 1993**

Name _____ Teacher _____ Grade Level _____ Score ____

Time Limit: 30 minutes | *Answer Column*

5-1.   If $A = 1990 \times 1991 \times 1992 \times 1993 \times 1994 \times 1995 \times 1996$ and $B = 1993^7$, which is larger, A or B?

5-1.

5-2.   If x, y, and z are unequal positive integers, what is the smallest possible value of a for which $x^1 + y^2 + z^3 = a$?

5-2.

5-3.   Solve for x: $\log_2(x + 1) = 2\log_2(x - 1)$.

5-3.

5-4.   The product of the first 23 positive integers, $1 \times 2 \times \ldots \times 22 \times 23$, can be written as the product of n consecutive positive integers in two ways for which $2 \le n \le 22$. What are these two values of n?

5-4.

5-5.   What are all real values of x which satisfy

$$\frac{\sqrt{21 + x} + \sqrt{21 - x}}{\sqrt{21 + x} - \sqrt{21 - x}} = \frac{21}{x}?$$

5-5.

5-6.   The bisector of any angle of a triangle divides the side opposite that angle into segments proportional to the other two sides. In the diagram, the bisector of an angle of the triangle shown divides the side opposite that angle into segments with lengths 2 and 5. If the perimeter of this triangle is an integer, what is the largest possible value of the perimeter?

5-6.

© 1993 by Mathematics Leagues Inc.

HIGH SCHOOL MATHEMATICS CONTESTS

Math League Press, P.O. Box 720, Tenafly, New Jersey 07670-0720

Contest Number 6   *Any calculator is always allowed.* Answers must be exact *or* have 4 (or more) significant digits, correctly rounded.   **April 6, 1993**

Name _____ Teacher _____ Grade Level ____ Score ____

Time Limit: 30 minutes   *Answer Column*

6-1. If $x^2 = y^2$, but $x \neq y$, what is the numerical value of $x^3 + y^3$?	6-1.
6-2. In a circle, the length of each of two parallel chords is 10. If the distance between these two chords is 24, what is the length of a diameter of this circle?	6-2.
6-3. What is the smallest positive degree-measure x for which $$(16^{\sin^2 x})(4^{2 \sin x})(2) = 1?$$	6-3.
6-4. If $0 < x < 1$, and the value of $\dfrac{1993}{x}$ is an *integer*, what is the least possible value of this integer?	6-4.
6-5. How many of the positive integers less than 10 000 contain the digit "1" at least once?	6-5.
6-6. If $x > y$, what is the ordered pair of real numbers (x,y) for which $$64^{2x} + 64^{2y} = 12 \text{ and } 64^{x+y} = 4\sqrt{2}?$$	6-6.

© 1993 by Mathematics Leagues Inc.

Solutions on Page 45 • Answers on Page 66   13

HIGH SCHOOL MATHEMATICS CONTESTS

Math League Press, P.O. Box 720, Tenafly, New Jersey 07670-0720

Contest Number 1   *Any calculator is always allowed.* Answers must be exact *or* have 4 (or more) significant digits, correctly rounded.   **November 2, 1993**

Name _____ Teacher _____ Grade Level ____ Score ____

Time Limit: 30 minutes | *Answer Column*

1-1.   My street address is a 3-digit number. If the product of the digits is 140, and the digits appear in increasing order from left to right, what is my street address? | 1-1.

1-2.   There is only one positive number a for which $x^2 + ax + 1993 = 0$ has two integral roots. What is this value of a? | 1-2.

1-3.   Four squares are lined up horizontally, as shown. The length of a side of the first square is 1. Each square after that has a side twice as long as a side of the previous square. What is the value of AB? | 1-3.

1-4.   How many ordered pairs of positive integers (a,c) satisfy the equation
$$a^3 + 64 = c^3?$$ | 1-4.

1-5.   The lengths of the sides of a right triangle are in the ratio 3:4:5. If the length of one of the three altitudes of this triangle is 60, what is the greatest possible area of this triangle? | 1-5.

1-6.   The set $\{1,2,3\}$ has $8 = 2^3$ different subsets: $\{1,2,3\}$, $\{1,2\}$, $\{1,3\}$, $\{2,3\}$, $\{1\}$, $\{2\}$, $\{3\}$, and $\{\ \}$. The set $\{1,2,3,4,5,6,7,8\}$ has $256 = 2^8$ different subsets. If Lee sums the elements in each subset of $\{1,2,3,4,5,6,7,8\}$, and then adds these 256 sums together, what total should Lee get? | 1-6.

© 1993 by Mathematics Leagues Inc.

HIGH SCHOOL MATHEMATICS CONTESTS

Math League Press, P.O. Box 720, Tenafly, New Jersey 07670-0720

Contest Number 2 *Any calculator is always allowed.* Answers must be exact *or* have 4 (or more) significant digits, correctly rounded. **December 7, 1993**

Name _____ Teacher _____ Grade Level _____ Score _____

Time Limit: 30 minutes   *Answer Column*

2-1. If the sum of two numbers is equal to their difference, what is their product? | 2-1.

2-2. Three integers a, b, and c are said to be in *arithmetic progression* if $c-b = b-a$. What are three different integers in arithmetic progression whose product is a positive prime? | 2-2.

2-3. On the circle shown at the right are marked the vertices of regular 20-sided polygon *ABCDEFGHIJKLMNOPQRST*. What is $m\angle CAT + m\angle DOG$? | 2-3.

2-4. What is the smallest positive integer divisible by 45 whose first four digits are 1993? | 2-4.

2-5. In $\triangle ABC$, $m\angle B = 90°$. The circle circumscribed about the triangle has a radius of length 10. The circle inscribed in the triangle is tangent to $\overline{AB}$ at D, to $\overline{BC}$ at E, and to $\overline{AC}$ at F. If the perimeter of the triangle is 42, what is $EB + BD$? | 2-5.

2-6. What are all ordered triples of real numbers (a,b,c) which satisfy $c^a = b^{2a}$, $2^c = 2(4^a)$, and $a + b + c = 10$. | 2-6.

© 1993 by Mathematics Leagues Inc.

Solutions on Page 47 • Answers on Page 66

HIGH SCHOOL MATHEMATICS CONTESTS

Math League Press, P.O. Box 720, Tenafly, New Jersey 07670-0720

Contest Number 3   *Any calculator is always allowed.* Answers must be exact *or* have 4 (or more) significant digits, correctly rounded.   **January 11, 1994**

Name _____ Teacher _____ Grade Level ____ Score ____

Time Limit: 30 minutes   *Answer Column*

3-1.	The sum of 10 consecutive odd integers is A. The sum of the *next* 10 consecutive odd integers is B. What is the value of $B - A$?	3-1.
3-2.	What are both values of x which satisfy $1994x^2 + x = 1993$?	3-2.
3-3.	A square is subdivided into two shaded rectangles and two unshaded squares, as shown at the right. A side of the larger unshaded square is 8 more than a side of the smaller. If the total area of the two unshaded squares is 1000, what is the total area of the two shaded rectangles?	3-3.
3-4.	If I begin flipping a fair coin repeatedly, what is the probability that I get three heads before I get two tails?	3-4.
3-5.	If $x \geq 0$ and $y \geq 0$, what are all ordered pairs (x,y) which satisfy $$3x = 7y \text{ and } x^3 = y^7?$$	3-5.
3-6.	I invested \$100. Each day, including the 1st day, my investment first increased in value by $p\%$, then decreased in value. The 1st day's decrease was one-quarter of the 1st day's increase. The 2nd day's decrease was two-quarters of the 2nd day's increase. In general, the nth day's decrease was n-quarters of the nth day's increase. (Note that, from day 5 on, the decrease exceeded the increase.) If my investment first had a value of 0 on the 1000th day, what was the value of p? [NOTE: In this problem, the words *increase* and *decrease* refer to the amount of increase or decrease, *not* the % of increase or decrease.]	3-6.

© 1994 by Mathematics Leagues Inc.

HIGH SCHOOL MATHEMATICS CONTESTS

Math League Press, P.O. Box 720, Tenafly, New Jersey 07670-0720

Contest Number 4   *Any calculator is always allowed.* Answers must be exact *or* have 4 (or more) significant digits, correctly rounded.   **February 8, 1994**

Name _____ Teacher _____ Grade Level _____ Score _____

Time Limit: 30 minutes   *Answer Column*

4-1. In the *addition* problem at the right, the ✿ and ∗ symbols both represent unknown digits. The various ∗ symbols may represent different digits. What digit is represented by the ✿ symbol?

```
    ∗ 3
    ∗ ∗
    ∗ ∗
    ∗ ∗
   ─────
   39 ✿
```

4-1.

4-2. Two externally tangent circles have radii of lengths 2 and 3 respectively. What is the length of a line segment drawn from the center of the smaller circle to the point at which the segment is tangent of the larger circle?

4-2.

4-3. Which of the following integers is the largest?

$$2^{3^5},\ 2^{5^3},\ 3^{2^5},\ 3^{5^2},\ 5^{2^3},\ 5^{3^2}$$

4-3.

4-4. A car traveling at 60 km/hr passed a person running at 12 km/hr and stopped after it reached Burger Queen, which was 4 km beyond the point where it passed the runner. How many minutes after the car reached Burger Queen did the runner reach Burger Queen?

4-4.

4-5. Pat said "I'm thinking of two numbers. One number is three times the other, and their sum is 8 more than twice the smaller number." What is the least possible number of which Pat was thinking?

4-5.

4-6. For what value of *n* are both of the following statements true?

If *n*+1 numbers are arbitrarily selected from the set {1, 2, 3, . . . ,1994}, there must be at least one pair whose sum is 1995. If only *n* numbers are selected, there may be no such pair.

4-6.

© 1994 by Mathematics Leagues Inc.

Solutions on Page 49 • Answers on Page 66   17

Contest Number 5   *Any calculator is always allowed.* Answers must be exact *or* have 4 (or more) significant digits, correctly rounded.   **March 8, 1994**

Name _____ Teacher _____ Grade Level ____ Score ____

Time Limit: 30 minutes | *Answer Column*

5-1.   If $a + b + c + d = 1992$ and $a + b = 1993$, what is the value of $1994c + 1994d$? | 5-1.

5-2.   In an isosceles triangle whose base is 30, the altitude to this base is 20. What is the length of an altitude drawn to one of the legs? | 5-2.

5-3.   Two line segments connect the points $A(1,3)$, $O(0,0)$, and $C(4,2)$, as shown at the right. What is the degree-measure of $\angle AOC$? | 5-3.

5-4.   What is the ordered pair of real numbers (a,b) for which the inequalities $2x \le y \le 5x$ and $ay \le x \le by$ are exactly equivalent? | 5-4.

5-5.   The product of two positive integers is 9984, and the greatest common factor of these integers equals the difference between them. What are the two integers? | 5-5.

5-6.   There is exactly one real number k for which the equation

$$(\log 3x)(\log 5x) = k$$

has only one real solution for x. What is this value of x? | 5-6.

© 1994 by Mathematics Leagues Inc.

Contest Number 6 — *Any calculator is always allowed.* Answers must be exact *or* have 4 (or more) significant digits, correctly rounded. — **April 12, 1994**

Name _____ Teacher _____ Grade Level _____ Score _____

Time Limit: 30 minutes | *Answer Column*

6-1. Three integers a, b, and c are said to be in *arithmetic progression* if $c-b = b-a$. Every item sold in a certain store has a price, in cents, that belongs to the arithmetic progression 7, 11, 15, 19, 23, 27, ... In cents, what is the least such price greater than 250?

6-1.

6-2. What are the three values of x for which
$$x^3 - x = 1994(x - 1)(x + 1)?$$

6-2.

6-3. A plane contains $\triangle AOB$ so that $\overline{AB}$ is the hypotenuse of right $\triangle ABC$ and $\overline{CO}$ is perpendicular to the plane. The legs of $\triangle ABC$ form angles of 45° and 30° with the plane, as shown. If the length of the shorter leg of $\triangle ABC$ is $\sqrt{3}$, how long is $\overline{AB}$?

6-3.

6-4. In increasing order, the numbers x^2, y^2, and z^2 are squares of consecutive positive integers. If $z^2 - x^2 = 888$, what is the value of y?

6-4.

6-5. A 12-sided polygon is inscribed in a circle of radius-length 1. What is the largest possible length of the shortest side of this polygon?

6-5.

6-6. If $f(x) = 1 - x - x^3$, what are all real values of x which satisfy
$$1 - f(x) - \left(f(x)\right)^3 > f(1 - 5x)?$$

6-6.

© 1994 by Mathematics Leagues Inc.

Solutions on Page 51 • Answers on Page 66

HIGH SCHOOL MATHEMATICS CONTESTS

Math League Press, P.O. Box 720, Tenafly, New Jersey 07670-0720

Contest Number 1 *Any calculator is always allowed.* Answers must be exact *or* have 4 (or more) significant digits, correctly rounded. **November 1, 1994**

Name _____ **Teacher** _____ **Grade Level** _____ **Score** _____

Time Limit: 30 minutes | *Answer Column*

1-1. If the sum of two prime numbers is 999, what is their product? | 1-1.

1-2. When my grandmother got married in 1950, both her age and her grandmother's age were respectively equal to the last two digits of their birth years! How old was my grandmother's grandmother when my grandmother got married? | 1-2.

1-3. If $\sqrt{17^2 + 17^2 + \ldots + 17^2} = 17^2$, how many times must 17^2 occur in the radicand on the left side of the equation? | 1-3.

1-4. Two perpendicular chords are drawn in a large circle, and two small circles are drawn, as shown, each tangent to the large circle and both chords. If the lengths of the radii of the two small circles are 3 and 4 respectively, what is the distance between their centers? | 1-4.

1-5. What is the value of x, rounded to the nearest integer, for which
$$\frac{1}{49} = \frac{2}{10^2} + \frac{4}{10^4} + \frac{8}{10^6} + \frac{16}{10^8} + \frac{32}{10^{10}} + \frac{x}{10^{12}} ?$$ | 1-5.

1-6. What is the sum of all integers x for which $\dfrac{3x + 25}{2x - 5}$ is an integer? | 1-6.

© 1994 by Mathematics Leagues Inc.

Contest Number 2   *Any calculator is always allowed.* Answers must be exact *or* have 4 (or more) significant digits, correctly rounded.   **December 6, 1994**

Name _____ Teacher _____ Grade Level ____ Score ____

Time Limit: 30 minutes   *Answer Column*

2-1.	The product of two numbers is equal to the product of their reciprocals. What are both possible values of this product?	2-1.
2-2.	Each side of square $ABCD$ has a length of 4, and each of the line segments $\overline{AF}$ and $\overline{DE}$ has a length of 5. What is the length of $\overline{EF}$?	2-2.
2-3.	"I see that our room numbers are 100 and 164," said Prof. Smart. "What of it?" retorted Prof. Clever. "If you add 125 to either number, you get a perfect square," replied Prof. Smart. After some time, Prof. Clever answered "There's an integer less than 125 that does the same thing." "You are wrong," said Prof. Smart. *Who was right: Prof. Smart or Prof. Clever?*	2-3.
2-4.	The roots of $x^2-26x+c = 0$ are r and s. If $19r+94s = 1994$, what is the value of c?	2-4.
2-5.	What are all real values of x which satisfy $\left\vert 2 - \left\vert 1 - \vert x \vert \right\vert \right\vert = 1$?	2-5.
2-6.	Quadrilateral $ABCD$ is drawn in a plane so that $AB = BC = CD$ and $AC = BD = AD$. What is $m\angle ABC$?	2-6.

© 1994 by Mathematics Leagues Inc.

Contest Number 3   *Any calculator is always allowed.* Answers must be exact *or* have 4 (or more) significant digits, correctly rounded.   **January 10, 1995**

Name _____ Teacher _____ Grade Level ____ Score ____

Time Limit: 30 minutes   *Answer Column*

3-1. Two consecutive price reductions of the same percent reduced the price of an item from $25 to $16. By what percent was the price reduced each time?	3-1.
3-2. What is the area of the smallest circle in which a pair of perpendicular chords can have lengths of 6 and 8?	3-2.
3-3. The difference between successive terms of an *arithmetic sequence* is constant. For example, 2, 5, 8, 11 is a four-term arithmetic sequence. After changing the value (but not the position) of one of the numbers 100, 140, 160, 170, 200, we'd still need one more number to have an ordered list of all six terms of an arithmetic sequence. What additional number is needed for us to have all six terms?	3-3.
3-4. One way to write 1995 as a product of three positive integers is to write $1995 = 7 \times 15 \times 19$. Altogether, for how many distinct ordered triples of positive integers (x,y,z), with $1 < x < y < z$, does $xyz = 1995$?	3-4.
3-5. What are all ordered pairs of real numbers (x,y) for which $$y^{x^2 - 7x + 12} = 1 \text{ and } x + y = 6?$$	3-5.
3-6. The diagonals of the trapezoid at the right divide the trapezoid into four triangles, as shown. If the areas of the two shaded triangles are 18 and 32, what is the area of the trapezoid?	3-6.

© 1995 by Mathematics Leagues Inc.

HIGH SCHOOL MATHEMATICS CONTESTS

Math League Press, P.O. Box 720, Tenafly, New Jersey 07670-0720

Contest Number 4 *Any calculator is always allowed.* Answers must be exact *or* have 4 (or more) significant digits, correctly rounded. **February 7, 1995**

Name _____ Teacher _____ Grade Level _____ Score _____

Time Limit: 30 minutes | *Answer Column*

4-1. If the lengths of two sides of a right triangle are 3 and 4, what is the least possible length of the third side?

4-1.

4-2. What is the integer n for which $5^n + 5^n + 5^n + 5^n + 5^n = 5^{25}$?

4-2.

4-3. If (6,9) and (10,3) are the coordinates of two opposite vertices of a square, what are the coordinates of the other two vertices?

4-3.

4-4. If i represents the imaginary unit, what is the ordered pair of real numbers (a,b) for which $(1 + i)^{13} = a + bi$?

4-4.

4-5. The diagram shows that an equiangular hexagon with side-lengths 6, 7, 9, 10, 11, and 14 can be inscribed in an equilateral triangle with side-length 30. This same equiangular hexagon can also be inscribed in an equilateral triangle with side-length $n \neq 30$. What is this value of n?

4-5.

4-6. In a certain sequence, the first number is 1995. The second number equals the first number divided by 1 more than the first number. The third number equals the second number divided by 1 more than the second number. From then on, each number in the sequence equals the previous number divided by 1 more than the previous number. What is the 1995th number in this sequence?

4-6.

© 1995 by Mathematics Leagues Inc.

HIGH SCHOOL MATHEMATICS CONTESTS

Math League Press, P.O. Box 720, Tenafly, New Jersey 07670-0720

Contest Number 5   *Any calculator is always allowed.* Answers must be exact *or* have 4 (or more) significant digits, correctly rounded.   **March 7, 1995**

Name _____ Teacher _____ Grade Level _____ Score _____

Time Limit: 30 minutes   *Answer Column*

5-1.   First form any positive integer n with fewer than 10 digits. Then,
- Let x be the number of even digits in n, let y be the number of odd digits in n, and let $z = x + y$.
- Replace n with the 3-digit number whose hundreds' digit is x (which may equal 0), whose tens' digit is y, and whose units' digit is z.

Repeat the two steps above 1995 times. What is the final value of n?

5-1.

5-2.   A square whose area is 16 is divided into 4 smaller squares. What is the area of the circle which passes through the centers of the four small squares?

5-2.

5-3.   When 270 is divided by the odd number x, the quotient is a positive prime (and the remainder is 0). What is the value of x?

5-3.

5-4.   If x is in radians, what is the only number x for which $\cos x = x$?

5-4.

5-5.   Pat tosses a fair coin, after which Lee throws a fair die. They continue this alternate coin-tossing and die-throwing until a head is tossed (in which case Pat wins) or a 2 is thrown (in which case Lee wins). What is the probability that Lee wins?

5-5.

5-6.   Write, in simplest form, all pairs of real numbers (x,y) for which

$$x^2 + x\sqrt[3]{xy^2} = 208, \text{ and}$$
$$y^2 + y\sqrt[3]{yx^2} = 1053.$$

5-6.

© 1995 by Mathematics Leagues Inc.

Contest Number 6   *Any calculator is always allowed.* Answers must be exact *or* have 4 (or more) significant digits, correctly rounded.   **April 11, 1995**

Name _____ Teacher _____ Grade Level _____ Score _____

Time Limit: 30 minutes   *Answer Column*

6-1. What are both real values of n for which $\sqrt{\sqrt{n}} = \sqrt{n}$?   6-1.

6-2. In a large equilateral triangle is inscribed a smaller one, its vertices at trisection points of sides of the larger, as shown. If the perimeter of the larger triangle is 9, what is the perimeter of the smaller equilateral triangle?   6-2.

6-3. What are all ordered pairs of integers (x,y), with $x < y$, for which   6-3.
$$x^2 + y^2 = 3^2 + 4^2?$$

6-4. What are all values of $x > 0$ for which $\log_{10} x = |\log_{10} x|$?   6-4.

6-5. In the ordered sequence of positive integers   6-5.

$$1, 2, 2, 3, 3, 3, 4, 4, 4, 4, \ldots ,$$

each positive integer n occurs in a block of n terms. For what value of k is the sum of the *reciprocals* of the first k terms equal to 1000?

6-6. In the diagram (which is *not* drawn to scale) squares are drawn on a leg and the hypotenuse of a right triangle, all in the same plane, as shown. If the area of square II is 19 and the area of square III is 95, what is the area of triangle I?   6-6.

© 1995 by Mathematics Leagues Inc.

Contest Number 1   *Any calculator is always allowed.* Answers must be exact *or* have 4 (or more) significant digits, correctly rounded.   **October 31, 1995**

Name _____ Teacher _____ Grade Level _____ Score _____

Time Limit: 30 minutes   *Answer Column*

1-1. What is the only pair of consecutive integers whose square roots are also consecutive integers?	1-1.
1-2. What is the ordered pair of integers (x, y) which satisfies $$36 \times 5^x = 225 \times 4^y?$$	1-2.
1-3. If a_m satisfies $\dfrac{a_m}{m+1} + m(m+1)^2 = \dfrac{1+a_m}{m}$, what is the value of a_4?	1-3.
1-4. My area code is a positive 3-digit number. Add 7 to it and the result is divisible by 7. Add 8 instead, and the result is divisible by 8. Add 9 instead, and the result is divisible by 9. What is my area code?	1-4.
1-5. In $\triangle ABC$, $PQ = \frac{1}{3}AB$, $RS = \frac{1}{5}AC$, and the area of $\triangle ABC$ is 1. If a is the sum of the areas of the darker shaded regions, and b is the sum of the areas of the lighter shaded regions, what is the value of $a - b$?	1-5.
1-6. On a straight road, an inspecting officer traveled from the rear to the front of an army column, and back, while the column marched forward its own length. If the officer and the column maintained steady (but different) speeds, what was the ratio of their speeds, faster to slower?	1-6.

© 1995 by Mathematics Leagues Inc.

Contest Number 2   *Any calculator is always allowed.* Answers must be exact *or* have 4 (or more) significant digits, correctly rounded.   **December 5, 1995**

Name _____ Teacher _____ Grade Level _____ Score _____

Time Limit: 30 minutes   *Answer Column*

2-1.   When the first 1995 positive odd primes are multiplied together, what is the units' digit of the product?

2-1.

2-2.   When $x = 10$, the expression $\sqrt{1 + 2 + 3 + x}$ has the value 4. What are all four integers $x < 10$ for which $\sqrt{1 + 2 + 3 + x}$ has an integral value?

2-2.

2-3.   Two squares are inscribed in a semicircle as shown. If the area of the smaller square is 25, what is the area of the larger square?

2-3.

2-4.   The College of Hard Knox belongs to a six-school league in which each school plays four games with each of the other schools. No tied games ever occur, and the other five schools finished this season having won, respectively, 20%, 30%, 35%, 60%, and 80% of the league games they played. What was the The College of Hard Knox's final winning record in the league this season (expressed as a percent)?

2-4.

2-5.   Place one *non-zero* digit in each box below so the resulting equation is true:

$$\boxed{}\boxed{}\% \text{ of } \boxed{}\boxed{}\boxed{} = 400.$$

2-5.
Put your answer in the shaded boxes at the left.

2-6.   Both x and y are positive numbers less than 2. Every positive number less than 2 is equally likely to be the value of x; and every positive number less than 2 is equally likely to be the value of y. What is the probability that x and y differ by less than 1?

2-6.

© 1995 by Mathematics Leagues Inc.

HIGH SCHOOL MATHEMATICS CONTESTS

Math League Press, P.O. Box 720, Tenafly, New Jersey 07670-0720

Contest Number 3

Any calculator is always allowed. Answers must be exact *or* have 4 (or more) significant digits, correctly rounded.

January 9, 1996

Name _____ Teacher _____ Grade Level _____ Score _____

Time Limit: 30 minutes

Answer Column

3-1   If $1996! = 1 \times \ldots \times 1996$, how many integers n satisfy the inequality

$$1996! + 19 < n < 1996! + 96?$$

3-1

3-2.   Three congruent squares are drawn as shown, in which the midpoints of two sides of the bottom squares are vertices of the top square. If $AB = 100$, what is the area of one of these squares?

3-2.

3-3.   What is largest number of (very small) checkers that could be placed on the accompanying 5×5 grid, so there is at most 1 checker on any small square, and there are at most 4 checkers in any column, in any row, and in any diagonal?

3-3.

3-4.   How many distinct pairs of positive integers (m,n) satisfy $m^n = 2^{20}$?

3-4.

3-5.   In the sequence 6, x, y, 16, the first three terms form an arithmetic progression, and the last three terms form a geometric progression. What are all possible ordered pairs (x,y)? [NOTE: The three numbers a, b, and c are said to be in *arithmetic progression* if $c - b = b - a$; but they are said to be in *geometric progression* if $\frac{c}{b} = \frac{b}{a}$.]

3-5.

3-6.   If a and b are positive integers and i is the imaginary unit, what is the only real number c for which

$$(a + bi)^4 - 24i = c?$$

3-6.

© 1996 by Mathematics Leagues Inc.

Solutions on Page 60 • Answers on Page 67

Contest Number 4 — *Any calculator is always allowed.* Answers must be exact *or* have 4 (or more) significant digits, correctly rounded. — **February 6, 1996**

Name _____ Teacher _____ Grade Level _____ Score _____

Time Limit: 30 minutes

Answer Column

4-1. Rufus and Dufus each took some money from a piggy bank to buy an ice cream cone, but Rufus was 24¢ short and Dufus was 2¢ short of the price of a cone They decided to pool their resources, but found they still could not afford to buy the cone. How many cents did the ice cream cone cost?

4-1.

4-2. The sum of three different numbers is 12. There are three different ways to pair the numbers, and the average of the numbers in such a pair is called a *pairwise average*. If $a, b,$ and c denote the pairwise averages of the three numbers, what is the average of a, b, and c?

4-2.

4-3. What are both real values of x which satisfy $1996^{1996} = x^{-1996}$?

4-3.

4-4. If $\sin\theta = 2\cos\theta$, what is the numerical value of $\cos^2\theta$?

4-4.

4-5. Each of three congruent circles has radius 1, and each is externally tangent to the other two. An equilateral triangle circumscribes this configuration, so that each circle is tangent to two of the sides of the triangle. What is the perimeter of the equilateral triangle?

4-5.

4-6. What is the least $n > 1$ for which the statement below is true?

In every *n*-element subset of the first 100 positive integers, at least one number is exactly divisible by another.

4-6.

© 1996 by Mathematics Leagues Inc.

HIGH SCHOOL MATHEMATICS CONTESTS

Math League Press, P.O. Box 720, Tenafly, New Jersey 07670-0720

Contest Number 5   *Any calculator is always allowed.* Answers must be exact *or* have 4 (or more) significant digits, correctly rounded.   **March 5, 1996**

Name _____ Teacher _____ Grade Level _____ Score _____

Time Limit: 30 minutes   *Answer Column*

5-1. The length of each side of a quadrilateral is 9. What is the largest possible area of the quadrilateral?	5-1.
5-2. There are exactly two ordered pairs of integers (a,b) which satisfy $a^3 = b^2 + 2$. One of these pairs is $(3,5)$. What is the other one?	5-2.
5-3. Lee will win a prize if Lee's guess of $\$G$ differs by no more than \$10 from the actual value of the prize, $\$P$. Write an inequality involving G and P which, if satisfied, and only if satisfied, indicates that Lee won the prize. The only restriction on your answer is that it must use exactly one inequality symbol and it must use it only once.	5-3.
5-4. What are all real numbers x which satisfy $\log_2\left(\dfrac{x-1}{x+1}\right) > 1$?	5-4.
5-5. The only series of consecutive whole numbers whose sum is 22 is $4+5+6+7$. What is the smallest number less than 1996 that is the first term of a series of consecutive whole numbers whose sum is 1996?	5-5.
5-6. Connect four 1×1 squares as shown to get the 5 pieces at the right, known as *tetrominoes*. Place these 5 tetrominoes inside a rectangle so the pieces do not overlap, and the sides of the pieces are on or are parallel to sides of the rectangle. If the sides of the rectangle have integer lengths, what is the least possible area of the rectangle?	5-6.

© 1996 by Mathematics Leagues Inc.

Contest Number 6   *Any calculator is always allowed.* Answers must be exact *or* have 4 (or more) significant digits, correctly rounded.   **April 16, 1996**

Name _____ Teacher _____ Grade Level ____ Score ____

Time Limit: 30 minutes   *Answer Column*

6-1.   What is the perimeter of the square which can be divided into rectangles whose areas are 9 and 16?   6-1.

6-2.   If $x = y^2$, what is the value of $y^{1996} - x^{998} + 499$?   6-2.

6-3.   When the transformation T, defined by $T(x,y) = (2x, 2y)$, is applied to each point of the graph of $y = \frac{16}{x}$, the resulting graph has the equation $y = \frac{k}{x}$. What is the value of k?   6-3.

6-4.   The lengths of the three altitudes of a right triangle are 12, 15, and 20. What is the length of the hypotenuse of this triangle?   6-4.

6-5.   What are all ordered pairs of numbers (x,y) which satisfy both   6-5.

$$x(x + y) = 9 \quad \text{and} \quad y(x + y) = 16?$$

6-6.   Ali writes some positive integers, all different, on stacks of paper. Each integer Ali writes is divisible by 2 and/or 3 but by no other prime. No matter how many numbers Ali writes, the sum of their reciprocals is always less than k. What is the least possible value of k?   6-6.

© 1996 by Mathematics Leagues Inc.

Complete Solutions
October, 1991 – April, 1996

Problem 1-1

Since $\sqrt{81} = x^2$, $x^2 = 9$, and $x = \boxed{\pm 3}$.

Problem 1-2

Since $10N = 10^N$ when $N = 1$, and $10N < 10^N$ for $N > 1$, the only positive integral solution is $N = \boxed{1}$.

Problem 1-3

Method I: Draw $\overline{AO}$, forming a 30°–60°–90° right triangle. Since the length of the leg opposite the 60° angle is $3\sqrt{3}$, the length of the radius is 6 and the area of the circle is $\boxed{36\pi}$.

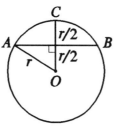

Method II: Instead of drawing radius $\overline{AO}$, extend $\overline{CO}$ its own length through O, forming a diameter. Since $\overline{AB}$ is split into two segments of length $3\sqrt{3}$, and the diameter is split into segments $\frac{r}{2}$ and $\frac{3r}{2}$, we have $(3\sqrt{3})(3\sqrt{3}) = \left(\frac{r}{2}\right)\left(\frac{3r}{2}\right)$. Solving, $r = 6$.

[**NOTE:** $\overline{AB}$ is a side of the equilateral triangle inscribed in the circle.]

Problem 1-4

Method I: We are told there is only one integral value of x for which $x^3 + (x+1)^3 + (x+2)^3 = (x+3)^3$, so we could expand both sides and solve the resulting cubic equation—but it's easier to first try substitution. If $x = 1$, $1+8+27 \neq 64$. If $x = 2$, $8+27+64 \neq 125$. If $x = 3$, $27+64+125 = 216$, so $x = \boxed{3}$.

Method II: Expanding the binomials and simplifying, we get $x^3 - 6x - 9 = 0$; the only rational root is 3.

Problem 1-5

Since $x > 1$, the only possible integral values of $\frac{6}{x}$ are 5, 4, 3, 2, 1. When we solve $\frac{6}{x} = 5, 4, 3, 2, 1$, the values of x are $\boxed{\frac{6}{5}, \frac{6}{4}, \frac{6}{3}, \frac{6}{2}, \frac{6}{1} \text{ or equivalents}}$.

[**NOTE:** This problem does **NOT** require that x is an integer; rather, it requires that $6/x$ is an integer.]

Problem 1-6

Method I: If $x \leq 0$ the left-hand side is positive, and there are no solutions. Therefore, $x > 0$. Add $3x$ to both sides. Since both sides are non-negative, square both sides to get $x^4 - 8x^2 + 16 \leq 9x^2 \Leftrightarrow x^4 - 17x^2 + 16 \leq 0 \Leftrightarrow (x^2 - 16)(x^2 - 1) \leq 0$. Since $x > 0$, the critical values are $x = 4$ and $x = 1$. Plotting these on the number line and testing the three resulting regions, we get $\boxed{1 \leq x \leq 4}$.

Method II: Since $0 \leq |x^2 - 4| \leq 3x$, graph $y = 3x$ and $y = |x^2 - 4|$ (by drawing $y = x^2 - 4$ and then reflecting, across the x-axis, that portion of $y = x^2 - 4$ that lies below the x-axis). The x-coordinates of the two points at which the graph of $y = |x^2 - 4|$ intersects the line $y = 3x$ are endpoints of the answer interval. The rightmost intersection point is at the positive solution of $x^2 - 4 = 3x$, where $x = 4$. The leftmost intersection point is at the positive solution of $4 - x^2 = 3x$, where $x = 1$. Hence, $1 \leq x \leq 4$.

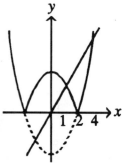

Method III: Use cases.

CASE I: If $|x^2 - 4| = x^2 - 4$, then $x \geq 2$ or $x \leq -2$. Solving $x^2 - 4 - 3x \leq 0$, we get $-2 \leq x \leq 4$. Taking the intersection, $2 \leq x \leq 4$.

CASE II: If $|x^2 - 4| = 4 - x^2$, then $-2 \leq x \leq 2$. Solving $4 - x^2 - 3x \leq 0$, we get $x \leq -4$ or $x \geq 1$. Taking the intersection, $1 \leq x \leq 2$.

Finally, the union of the two intervals $1 \leq x \leq 2$ and $2 \leq x \leq 4$ is the interval $1 \leq x \leq 4$.

Contests written and compiled by Steven R. Conrad & Daniel Flegler   **Mathematics Leagues Inc., © 1991**

Problem 2-1

The number 81 has five positive integral divisors: 1, 3, 9, 27, 81. Since $a+b+c+d = 20$, $a,b,c,d \le 9$. Two divisors are 9, the other two are 1, and the answer is $\boxed{(1,9,9,1) \text{ or any rearrangement of these four integers}}$.

Problem 2-2

The hypotenuse will be minimized when the legs are equal in length. When the length of each leg is 10, the length of the hypotenuse is $\boxed{10\sqrt{2} \text{ or } \sqrt{200}}$.

Problem 2-3

Method I: Adding terms, $15x = \frac{15k}{8}$; so $\frac{x}{k} = \boxed{\frac{1}{8}}$.

Method II: Since $x(1+2+4+8) = \frac{k}{8}(1+2+4+8)$, it follows that $x = \frac{k}{8}$, so $\frac{x}{k} = \frac{1}{8}$.

Problem 2-4

If we subtract the first equation from the second, we get $2x+2y+2z+2w = -4$; so $x+y+z+w = \boxed{-2}$.

Problem 2-5

Method I: In the diagram below, the three given vertices of the parallelogram are the dark circles; they are connected to form the inner triangle. These points are the midpoints of the sides of the larger triangle drawn at the right. By using any one of the vertices of this large 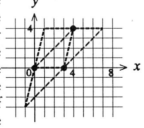 triangle as its fourth vertex, three parallelograms can be completed, as illustrated. The coordinates of these three points are $\boxed{(-1,-4), (1,4), (7,4)}$.

Method II: Since the diagonals of a parallelogram have the same midpoint, four different points can serve as the vertices of a parallelogram if and only if pairs of opposite vertices have equal x-coordinate sums and equal y-coordinate sums. Label the points $O(0,0)$, $A(3,0)$, $B(4,4)$, and $P(x,y)$. If points O and A are opposite vertices, then $0+3 = 4+x$ and $0+0 = 4+y$, so $(x,y) = (-1,-4)$. If O and B are opposite vertices, then $0+4 = 3+x$ and $0+4 = 0+y$, so $(x,y) = (1,4)$. If O and P are opposite vertices, then $0+x = 3+4$ and $0+y = 0+4$, so $(x,y) = (7,4)$.

Problem 2-6

Let $f(x) = \frac{1}{x-1} + \frac{1}{x-2} + \frac{1}{x-3}$. If $x < 1$, then $f(x)$ is negative. If $x > 3$, then $f(x)$ is positive. We know that f is undefined at $x = 1, 2,$ and 3. Elsewhere, f is the sum of the reciprocals of three increasing functions. Hence, f is a decreasing function—and the graph of $y = f(x)$ appears at the right. Note that 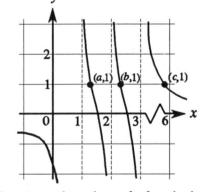 the solutions of $f(x) \ge 1$ are the values of x for which the graph of $y = f(x)$ is on or above $y = 1$. The line $y = 1$ intersects $y = f(x)$ three times. Let a, b, c be the roots of $f(x) = 1$, with $1 < a < 2 < b < 3 < c$. The solution intervals are $(1,a]$, $(2,b]$, $(3,c]$; and the sum of their lengths is $(a-1)+(b-2)+(c-3) = (a+b+c)-6$. But a, b, c are roots of $f(x) = 1$. Without separately calculating each individual root, we can still determine the sum $a+b+c$: Recall that $f(x) = 1 \Leftrightarrow \frac{1}{x-1} + \frac{1}{x-2} + \frac{1}{x-3} = 1$. Clearing fractions, $3x^2 -12x+11 = x^3-6x^2+11x-6$. Simplifying, we get $x^3- 9x^2+23x-17 = 0$. Since the sum of the roots of any cubic equation is the *opposite* of the coefficient of x^2, divided by the coefficient of x^3; we know that $a+b+c = 9$. Finally, the answer is $9-6 = \boxed{3}$.

Contests written and compiled by Steven R. Conrad & Daniel Flegler   **Mathematics Leagues Inc., © 1991**

Problem 3-1

For the sum to be 1992, all but one of the integers must be 1's. The remaining one must be a $\boxed{2}$.

Problem 3-2

Simplifying, $\frac{1}{x^2} = \frac{4^2+3^2}{3^2 \times 4^2} = \frac{5^2}{12^2}$, so $x = \boxed{\frac{12}{5}}$.

[**NOTE:** The above shows that, whenever a and b are the "legs" of a Pythagorean triple, then the equation $a^{-2}+b^{-2} = c^{-2}$ has a rational solution for c.]

Problem 3-3

Since the area of this triangle is 1, $\frac{1}{2}|ab| = 1$, or $|ab| = 2$. The possible values of a are: $\boxed{1,-1,2,-2}$.

Problem 3-4

Method I: If a is an integer, then $36a+1$ is very close in value to $36a$. If $3a^2 = 36a$, then $a = 0$ or 12. Since a is a positive integer, $a = \boxed{12}$.

Method II: The real roots of $36a+1 = 3a^2$ are given by $a = \frac{1}{6}\left(36 \pm \sqrt{36^2-4(3)(-1)}\right) \approx 6 \pm 6.0277$. The positive integer most nearly equal to a root is 12.

Problem 3-5

Method I: One zero is $x = \sqrt{2}+\sqrt{7}$. Squaring both sides, $x^2 = 9+2\sqrt{14}$. Rearranging and squaring, we get $(x^2-9)^2 = 4\times14 = 56$. Simplifying, $x^4-18x^2+25 = 0$. Therefore, $P(x) = x^4-18x^2+25$. It can be proven that this is the only P which works; so $P(1)$ is uniquely determined, and $P(1) = 1-18+25 = \boxed{8}$.

Method II: It can be proven that the other three zeros are $-\sqrt{2}-\sqrt{7}$, $\sqrt{2}-\sqrt{7}$, and $-\sqrt{2}+\sqrt{7}$. Therefore,
$$f(x) = (x-\sqrt{2}-\sqrt{7})(x+\sqrt{2}+\sqrt{7})(x-\sqrt{2}+\sqrt{7})(x+\sqrt{2}-\sqrt{7})$$
$$= \left(x^2-(\sqrt{2}+\sqrt{7})^2\right)\left(x^2-(\sqrt{2}-\sqrt{7})^2\right); \text{ and, finally,}$$
$$f(1) = \left(1-(9+2\sqrt{14})\right)\left(1-(9-2\sqrt{14})\right)$$
$$= (-8-2\sqrt{14})(-8+2\sqrt{14})$$
$$= 64-4\times14 = 64-56 = 8.$$

Problem 3-6

Draw an altitude from B to $\overline{AE}$; and also draw an altitude from C to $\overline{AE}$. Since $\triangle APB$ and $\triangle EPB$ both have the same altitude from B, the ratio of their areas = the ratio of their bases = $\frac{AP}{EP}$. Since $\triangle APC$ and $\triangle EPC$ both have the same altitude from C, the ratio of their areas $= \frac{40+30}{35} = \frac{2}{1} =$ the ratio of their bases $= \frac{AP}{EP}$; so if the area of $\triangle EPB$ is k, then

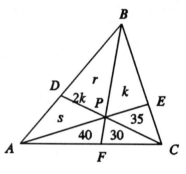

the area of $\triangle APB$ is $2k$. Next, $\triangle BPC$ and $\triangle FPC$ have the same altitude from C, and $\triangle BPA$ and $\triangle FPA$ have the same altitude from A; so, their areas ratios are both $\frac{BP}{FP}$. Thus, $\frac{k+35}{30} = \frac{2k}{40}$. Solving, $k = 70$. Let the area of $\triangle DPB = r$ and that of $\triangle DPA = s$. The area ratio of $\triangle DPB$ to $\triangle CPB = \frac{r}{35+70} =$ the area ratio of $\triangle DPA$ to $\triangle CPA = \frac{s}{30+40}$; so $\frac{r}{s} = \frac{3}{2}$. Since $r + s = 2k = 140$, $s = 56$, and $r = \boxed{84}$.

Contests written and compiled by Steven R. Conrad & Daniel Flegler   Mathematics Leagues Inc., © 1992

Problem 4-1

Method I: The original equation is equivalent to the equation $\left(\frac{1}{3}\right)^n + \left(\frac{2}{3}\right)^n = 1$. If $n \leq 0$, the left side exceeds 1. If $n > 1$, the left side is smaller than 1. The two sides are equal, however, when $n = \boxed{1}$.

Method II: If $n \leq 0$, $1^n + 2^n > 1$, while $3^n \leq 1$; so no solutions exist for $n \leq 0$. The binomial theorem assures us that, for $n > 1$, $1^n + 2^n < (1+2)^n = 3^n$; so there are no solutions for $n > 1$. Finally, when $n = 1$, $1^n + 2^n = 3^n$.

Problem 4-2

It is easy to see that $6 = 2 \times 3$, $8 = 2 \times 4$, and $12 = 3 \times 4$, so the lengths of the edges are 2, 3, and 4; and the volume of the solid is $2 \times 3 \times 4 = \boxed{24}$.

Problem 4-3

Method I: If you notice that $x(x+1) = (1991)(1992) = (-1992)(-1991)$, then $x = \boxed{1991, -1992}$.

Method II: The equation $x^2 + x - 1991 \times 1992 = 0$ factors into $(x+1992)(x-1991) = 0$. Now, solve.

Problem 4-4

Method I: All such sums are equal (to be proven in Method II below), so find *any* set of numbers which works and its sum is the answer. The numbers along the diagonal 1, 17, . . . , 225 meet the requirements of the problem. Their sum is $\frac{15}{2}(1+225) = \boxed{1695}$.

Method II: In one row, the chosen number is from the left column. In a 2nd row (not necessarily the 2nd row from the top), the chosen number is from the 2nd column, so it is 1 more than the number in the left column of that row. In a 3rd row the chosen number is from the 3rd column, so it is 2 more than the number in the left column of that row—etc. The sum of the chosen numbers equals the sum of the numbers in the left column + $(1+2+3+\ldots+14)$.

Problem 4-5

In $30°-60°-90°$ $\triangle ABC$, if $BC = r$, then $AB = 2r$ and the diameter of the large circle is $3r$. The area of the small circle is πr^2. The area of the large circle is $9\pi r^2$. The $60°$ sector is $\frac{1}{6}$ of that, so the required ratio is $\boxed{2:3}$.

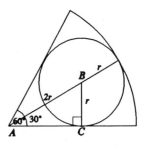

Problem 4-6

Method I: Let $u = \sqrt{x^2 + x + 1}$ and $v = \sqrt{x^2 - x + 1}$. We know that $u+v = 4$. But $u^2 - v^2 = 2x$. Dividing, $u-v = \frac{x}{2}$. Since $u+v = 4$, $u = \frac{x}{4}+2$. Squaring and substituting x^2+x+1 for u^2, $x^2+x+1 = \frac{x^2}{16}+x+4$. Simplifying, $x^2 = \frac{16}{5}$. The positive value of x is $\boxed{\frac{4}{\sqrt{5}}}$.

Method II: Let $y = x^2-x+1$. Then, $\sqrt{y+2x} + \sqrt{y} = 4$. Squaring, $2y+2x+2\sqrt{y(y+2x)} = 8$. Divide by 2, isolate the radical, and square: $y(y+2x) = (8-y-x)^2$. Square, collect terms, simplify: $x^2 = \frac{16}{5}$, so $x = \frac{4}{\sqrt{5}}$.

Method III: Rationalizing the left side's *numerator*,

$$\frac{\sqrt{x^2+x+1} + \sqrt{x^2-x+1}}{1} \times \frac{\sqrt{x^2+x+1} - \sqrt{x^2-x+1}}{\sqrt{x^2+x+1} - \sqrt{x^2-x+1}} = 4, \text{ or}$$

$$\frac{(x^2+x+1) - (x^2-x+1)}{\sqrt{x^2+x+1} - \sqrt{x^2-x+1}} = \frac{2x}{\sqrt{x^2+x+1} - \sqrt{x^2-x+1}} = 4.$$ Dividing by 2, $x = 2\left(\sqrt{x^2+x+1} - \sqrt{x^2-x+1}\right)$. But, $8 = 2\left(\sqrt{x^2+x+1} + \sqrt{x^2-x+1}\right)$. Adding these two equations, $x+8 = 4\sqrt{x^2+x+1}$. Now, square and solve.

Contests written and compiled by Steven R. Conrad & Daniel Flegler

Mathematics Leagues Inc., © 1992

Problem 5-1

Since $x^2-y^2 = (x+y)(x-y) = 5$, $2^{x^2-y^2} = 2^5 = \boxed{32}$.

Problem 5-2

In a $30°-60°-90°$ triangle, if the length of the shortest side is x, the length of the longest side is $2x$. Since $2x-x = 1992$, $x = 1992$, and $2x = \boxed{3984}$.

Problem 5-3

Method I: Since $\sec^2 x = 1+\tan^2 x$, $2\tan^2 x+1 = 1$, so $\tan x = 0$. The least positive value of x is $\boxed{\pi}$.

Method II: Since $\sec^2 x \geq 1$, $\tan x = 0$ and $x = \pi$.

Problem 5-4

Method I: If we let $y = x^5$, then $y^2+y-1056 = 0$. Since $2^5 = 32$ is one value of $y = x^5$, we can factor as $(y-32)(y+33) = 0$. Thus, $y = x^5 = \boxed{32, -33}$.

Method II: Since $x^5(x^5+1) = 2^5(2^5+1) = (32)(33) = (-33)(-32)$, $x^5 = 32$ or -33.

Problem 5-5

Acceptable numbers all look like $32xxx$, $n32xx$, $nx32x$, or $nxx32$, where n and x are digits, $n \neq 0$. There are $10^3 = 1000$ numbers of the first type and $9 \times 10^2 = 900$ of the other three types, for a total (so far) of 3700 numbers. Some of these 3700 numbers have been counted twice, so we must eliminate the repetitions. Numbers counted twice are of the form $3232x$, or $32x32$, or $n3232$; and there are $10+10+9 = 29$ such duplicates. Subtracting, $3700-29 = \boxed{3671}$.

Problem 5-6

First, since the sum of the roots is $a+1$ and both roots are negative, $a+1 < 0$; or $a < -1$. Next, the product of the roots is $a+4$, so $a+4 > 0$; or $a > -4$. Finally, the roots are real, so the discriminant must be non-negative. Hence, $a^2-2a-15 \geq 0$, from which $a \leq -3$ or $a \geq 5$. Taking the intersection of all three requirements, the roots will be negative precisely when $\boxed{-4 < a \leq -3}$.

Contests written and compiled by Steven R. Conrad & Daniel Flegler   Mathematics Leagues Inc., © 1992

Problem 6-1

Method I: Subtracting the left side from the right side, $x+y = 0$, so $x = -y$ and $\frac{x}{y} = \boxed{-1}$.

Method II: Dividing by y, $1991(\frac{x}{y})+1991 = 1992 \times (\frac{x}{y}+1)$. Now, solve for $\frac{x}{y}$.

Problem 6-2

Method I: Make one list of ages starting with 14 and a second list starting with 41. Simultaneously, go down the lists one year at a time until the father is 52 and Brian is $\boxed{25}$.

Method II: Let $10t+u$ = the father's age and $10u+t$ = Brian's age. Brian is 27 years younger than his father, so $10t+u = 10u+t+27$. Simplifying, $t-u = 3$. Currently, $u = 1$ and $t = 4$. The next digit reversal will occur when $u = 2$ and $t = 5$, when Brian is 25.

Problem 6-3

Draw the other diagonal of the quadrilateral (represented in the accompanying diagram by a dotted line). This creates two isosceles triangles each of whose bases has a length of 16 and whose altitudes have respective lengths of 6 and 15. Finally, the area of the original quadrilateral equals the sum of the areas of these two triangles = $\frac{1}{2}(16)(6)+\frac{1}{2}(16)(15) = \boxed{168}$.

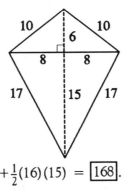

Problem 6-4

Since $x > 0$, $4^{100} < 8^x \Leftrightarrow 2^{200} < 2^{3x} \Leftrightarrow 200 < 3x$. The least positive integer value of x is $\boxed{67}$.

Problem 6-5

Method I: Since $\log_5 x = \frac{\log x}{\log 5}$ and $\log_x 5 = \frac{\log 5}{\log x}$, we know that $\log_5 x$ and $\log_x 5$ are reciprocals. The only numbers which are their own reciprocals are 1 and -1. Therefore, $\log_5 x = \pm 1$, so $x = \boxed{5, \frac{1}{5}}$.

Method II: Rewrite the equation as $\frac{\log x}{\log 5} = \frac{\log 5}{\log x}$, from which $\log^2 x = \log^2 5$. If $\log x = \log 5$, then $x = 5$. If $\log x = -\log 5 = \log \frac{1}{5}$, then $x = \frac{1}{5}$.

Problem 6-6

Method I: Rationalizing the denominator of the second fraction and then adding the fractions, we get $7+\sqrt{x}+\frac{5+\sqrt{x}}{25-x} = \frac{180-7x+\sqrt{x}\,(26-x)}{25-x}$. Since x is an integer but not a perfect square, this expression will be irrational unless $(26-x) = 0$, or $x = \boxed{26}$.

Method II: Adding the fractions and simplifying the result, $\frac{(36-x)-2\sqrt{x}}{5-\sqrt{x}} = q$, a rational number. Clearing fractions, $(36-x)-2\sqrt{x} = (5q)-q\sqrt{x}$. Equating coefficients of the rational and irrational parts, $36-x = 5q$ and $2\sqrt{x} = q\sqrt{x}$. From this last equation, $q = 2$. Substituting, $36-x = 10$, so $x = 26$.

Method III: $7+\sqrt{x}+\frac{1}{5-\sqrt{x}}$ will be rational if and only if it is equal to its conjugate, $7-\sqrt{x}+\frac{1}{5+\sqrt{x}}$. Equating these two expressions and clearing fractions, we get $(7+\sqrt{x})(25-x)+5+\sqrt{x} = (7-\sqrt{x})(25-x)+5-\sqrt{x}$. Simplifying, $2\sqrt{x}+(25-x)(2\sqrt{x}) = 0$. Factoring this equation, $\sqrt{x}(52-2x) = 0$. Since x is ot the square of an integer, $x \neq 0$, so $x = 26$.

Contests written and compiled by Steven R. Conrad & Daniel Flegler   Mathematics Leagues Inc., © 1992

Problem 1-1

For each number $\frac{a}{b}$ that Jack wrote, Jill wrote the number $\frac{b}{a}$. Exactly one number in each such pair is between 0 and 1, and half of 200 is $\boxed{100}$.

Problem 1-2

By the Pythagorean Theorem, $n + (n+1) = n+2$. Solving, $n = \boxed{1}$.

Problem 1-3

Method I: As seen in the diagram, the number of triangles needed is $1 + 3 + 5 + \ldots + 15 + 17 + 19 = \boxed{100}$.

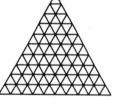

Method II: The area of an equilateral triangle with side s is $\frac{s^2\sqrt{3}}{4}$. Computing areas, it takes 100 of the smaller triangles to fill the large triangle.

Method III: The ratio of the areas of two similar figures is the square of the ratio of corresponding linear dimensions. Since the linear dimensions are in the ratio 10:1, the areas are in the ratio 100:1.

Problem 1-4

Method I: Squaring, $1992 = 1992^2 x$, so $x = \boxed{\dfrac{1}{1992}}$.

Method II: Since $\sqrt{x} = \frac{\sqrt{1992}}{1992} = \frac{1}{\sqrt{1992}}$, $x = \frac{1}{1992}$.

Problem 1-5

Method I: To declare a champion, whichever team wins the first game must then win the next three games. Since either team may win the first game, the required probability is $1 \times \frac{1}{2} \times \frac{1}{2} \times \frac{1}{2} = \boxed{\dfrac{1}{8}}$.

Method II: Call the teams A and B. The probability that A wins 4 games in a row is $\left(\frac{1}{2}\right)^4 = \frac{1}{16}$. The probability B does this is $\left(\frac{1}{2}\right)^4 = \frac{1}{16}$. The probability that *either* team wins 4 in a row is $\frac{1}{16} + \frac{1}{16} = \frac{1}{8}$.

Problem 1-6

We can't pay a price of $1, $2, $3, $4, or $5 using only $6 and/or $11 bills. Let's look at an item whose price we *can* pay. In the set of bills used as payment, if there's even one $11 bill, we could replace it with two $6 bills to show how to pay for an item that costs $1 more. Thus, if payment for an item costing $D includes one or more $11 bills, an item costing $(D+1) can be bought with only $6 and/or $11 bills. We *might* have a problem paying the $(D+1) price if the $D payment uses only $6 bills. In that case, if we have *a lot* of $6 bills, we could replace nine $6 bills (valued at $54) with five $11 bills (valued at $55) to pay for an item costing $(D+1). Thus, if we have nine or more $6 bills, and/or one or more $11 bills, we can pay for an item costing $1 more—then $1 more than that, then $1 more than that, and so on, forever! What $(D+1) amounts *cannot* be paid? If the $D payment includes only $6 bills, but includes fewer than nine $6 bills, then we can't pay $(D+1). To obtain the largest impossible price, let the $D amount be $48, which can be paid with eight $6 bills. We cannot now pay a price that is exactly $1 more. Since we can pay a $50 price with one $6 bill and four $11 bills—and then pay any price increase from then on—the largest whole number of dollars which could *not* be the price of an item is $\boxed{49 \text{ or } \$49}$.

Contests written and compiled by Steven R. Conrad & Daniel Flegler   Mathematics Leagues Inc., © 1992

Problem 2-1

Since $-3 + (-2) + (-1) + 0 + 1 + 2 + 3 + 4 + 5 = 9$ shows how to write 9 as the sum of 9 consecutive integers, and one term is 0, the product of these 9 integers is $\boxed{0}$.

Problem 2-2

Method I: Since $x^2 - 25x + 144 = (x-16)(x-9)$, the sum of the factors of $x^2 - 25x + 144$ is $2x - 25$. Since $x^2 - 26x + 144 = (x-18)(x-8)$, the sum of the factors of $x^2 - 26x + 144$ is $2x - 26$. Subtracting the second sum from the first, the result is $\boxed{1}$.

Method II: The sum of the factors $(x-a)$ and $(x-b)$ is $2x - (a+b) = 2x - $ (sum of the roots). The sum of the roots of $x^2 - px + q = 0$ is p, so, without actually factoring, the result we seek is $(-25) - (-26) = 1$.

Problem 2-3

For $x < 0$, the expression equals $3|x| = \boxed{1992}$.

Problem 2-4

$\frac{2x-1}{x+1} \le 1 \Leftrightarrow \frac{2x-1}{x+1} - 1 \le 0 \Leftrightarrow \frac{x-2}{x+1} \le 0$. For the last inequality, the critical values are $x = -1$ and $x = 2$. If $x < -1$, both $x-2$ and $x+1$ are negative, so their quotient is positive. At $x = -1$, the quotient is undefined. If $x > 2$, both $x-2$ and $x+1$ are positive, so their quotient is positive. The values of x which satisfy $\frac{x-2}{x+1} \le 0$, x are in the interval $\boxed{-1 < x \le 2}$.

Problem 2-5

The radicand of $\sqrt{6x - x^2 - 9} = \sqrt{-(x^2 - 6x + 9)} = \sqrt{-(x-3)^2}$ is negative unless $x = 3$. But, when the radicand is negative, y is imaginary. And, when $x = 3$, $y = 0$. The distance from $(0,0)$ to $(3,0)$ is $\boxed{3}$.

Problem 2-6

If we let the circles with centers A and B have respective radii R and r, then,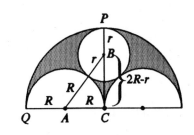

$QC = 2R$. We get the shaded region by removing the regions bounded by the small circle and the congruent semicircles from the region bounded by the large semicircle. Therefore, we can write the equation $45\pi = \frac{\pi(2R)^2}{2} - 2\left(\frac{\pi R^2}{2}\right) - \pi r^2 = \pi(R^2 - r^2)$. To solve this equation for r, we must first express R in terms of r. Since $CB = CP - BP = 2R-r$, in right $\triangle ABC$ we can write $(R+r)^2 = R^2 + (2R-r)^2$. Expanding and simplifying, $6Rr = 4R^2$, so $R = \frac{3r}{2}$. When we substitute into the equation 5 lines above, we get $45\pi = \pi\left(\frac{9r^2}{4} - \frac{4r^2}{4}\right)$, $r^2 = 36$, and $r = \boxed{6}$.

[**NOTE:** $\triangle ABC$ is a 3:4:5 triangle!]

Contests written and compiled by Steven R. Conrad & Daniel Flegler

Mathematics Leagues Inc., ©1992

Problem 3-1

Method I: We know that $\sqrt{n^2}$ is always an integer. For $\sqrt{n^2+1}$ to also be an integer, it would have to be exactly 1 more than $\sqrt{n^2}$. The difference between any two of the perfect squares 0, 1, 4, 9, ... is greater than 1 unless $\sqrt{n^2} = |n| = \boxed{0}$.

Method II: Let $\sqrt{n^2+1} = m$. If we square and rearrange, $m^2-n^2 = (m+n)(m-n) = (1)(1)$ or $(-1)(-1)$. In each case, $n = 0$.

Problem 3-2

Expanding and simplifying, $x^2-1993x = x(x-1993) = 0$. Solving, $x = \boxed{0, 1993}$.

Problem 3-3

Since the diagonals of a parallelogram bisect each other, and one side of the parallelogram is 13, the diagonals of the parallelogram are perpendicular. The parallelogram is a rhombus whose perimeter is $4 \times 13 = \boxed{52}$.

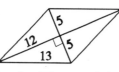

Problem 3-4

Method I: The "magic" sum is the sum of 7 entries from the magic square. The average entry is 25, so the "magic" sum is $7 \times 25 = \boxed{175}$.

Method II: Use the diagram. The answer is 175.

30	39	48	1	10	19	28
38	47	7	9	18	27	29
46	6	8	17	26	35	37
5	14	16	25	34	36	45
13	15	24	33	42	44	4
21	23	32	41	43	3	12
22	31	40	49	2	11	20

Method III: The sum of the positive integers from 1 through 49 is $\frac{49}{2}(1+49)$. This represents the sum of the entries in 7 rows. One-seventh of this sum is 175.

Problem 3-5

Since 97 is a prime, and 101 is the next prime, there are exactly 25 primes less than 98, 99, 100, and 101. The number of such values *other* than 100 is $\boxed{3}$.

[**NOTE:** The first 25 primes are 2, 3, 5, 7, 11, 13, 17, 19, 23, 29, 31, 37, 41, 43, 47, 53, 59, 61, 67, 71, 73, 79, 83, 89, and 97.]

Problem 3-6

Let $a = x^2$ and $b = y^2$, making $a > 0$ and $b > 0$. The original equation becomes $a^2 + b^2 = a + b$, or $(a^2-a) + (b^2-b) = 0$. Completing the squares, $(a-\frac{1}{2})^2 + (b-\frac{1}{2})^2 = \frac{1}{2}$. To make x as large as possible, make a as large as possible. To make a as large as possible, make $(a-\frac{1}{2})^2$ as large as possible. To make $(a-\frac{1}{2})^2$ as large as possible, make $(b-\frac{1}{2})^2$ as small as possible. Since the smallest possible value of $(b-\frac{1}{2})^2$ is 0, the largest possible value of $(a-\frac{1}{2})^2$ is $\frac{1}{2}$. Solving for a, $a-\frac{1}{2} = \frac{\sqrt{2}}{2}$, $a = \frac{1+\sqrt{2}}{2}$, and $x = \boxed{\sqrt{\frac{1+\sqrt{2}}{2}}}$.

[**NOTE:** Of course, $x = 1.099$ is also acceptable!]

Contests written and compiled by Steven R. Conrad & Daniel Flegler   **Mathematics Leagues Inc., © 1993**

Problem 4-1

Since $2^0 = 1$, $x = 3$. Since $5^0 = 1$, $y = -2$. Therefore, $2^x 5^y = 2^3 5^{-2} = \boxed{\dfrac{8}{25}}$.

Problem 4-2

One of the integers must be 0, so the largest that one of the 1993 consecutive integers could be is $\boxed{1992}$.

Problem 4-3

Clearly $N > 1$. Also, $3^{50} \approx 7.179 \times 10^{23}$ is too large, since it is a 24-digit number. Finally, $2^{50} \approx 1.126 \times 10^{15}$, 2^{50} is a 16-digit number, so $N = \boxed{2}$.

Problem 4-4

Method I: For **any** value of x from -2 to 3, the value of $|x+2| + |x-3|$ is 5. So, from $x = -2$ to $x = 3$, $y = |x+2| + |x-3|$ has the same graph as $y = 5$. The region we want is a square whose area is $\boxed{25}$.

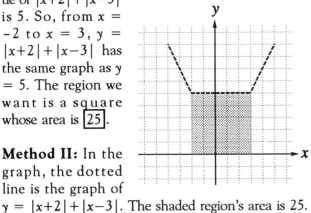

Method II: In the graph, the dotted line is the graph of $y = |x+2| + |x-3|$. The shaded region's area is 25.

Problem 4-5

In the diagram, the sides of the square are 12. Let the segments of the hypotenuse be x and $65-x$. Since tangents drawn to a circle from the same outside point are congruent, two segments have length x and two have length $65 - x$. The perimeter of the triangle is $24 + 2(65 - x) + 2x = \boxed{154}$.

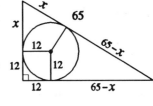

Problem 4-6

We know that $\dfrac{\langle x \rangle}{[x]} = \dfrac{[x]}{x}$, with $x > 0$. From these conditions, we conclude that $[x] \neq 0$, so $\langle x \rangle \neq 0$. Recall that $\langle x \rangle$ is fractional, with $0 < \langle x \rangle < 1$, and $[x]$ is integral.

Method I: Clearing fractions, we get $x\langle x \rangle = [x]^2$. Let's try to determine the value of $[x]$. If $[x] = 2$, the value of the right side of the equation in the first line (of this Method) would be 4. What about the left side? If $[x] = 2$, then $2 \leq x < 3$. Since $\langle x \rangle$ is a fraction between 0 and 1, the left side of the equation would be less than 3. Hence, $[x] \neq 2$. If $[x] > 2$, the difference between the values of the two sides would grow even larger, so $[x] = 1$. Since $[x] + \langle x \rangle = x$, we get $\langle x \rangle = x - 1$. Substituting into $x\langle x \rangle = [x]^2$, we get $x(x - 1) = 1^2$. Solving, $x = \boxed{\dfrac{1+\sqrt{5}}{2}}$.

Method II: Taking reciprocals of the equation in the very first line of this solution, above Method I, we get
$$\frac{[x]}{\langle x \rangle} = \frac{x}{[x]} \Leftrightarrow \frac{[x]}{\langle x \rangle} = \frac{[x] + \langle x \rangle}{[x]} \Leftrightarrow \frac{[x]}{\langle x \rangle} = 1 + \frac{\langle x \rangle}{[x]}.$$
We can use this last equation to determine the value of $[x]$. Recall that $0 < \langle x \rangle < 1$. If $[x] \geq 2$, the right side would be less than 2, but the left side would be greater than 2. Therefore, $[x] = 1$. Solving $1 + \langle x \rangle = \dfrac{1}{\langle x \rangle}$, $\langle x \rangle = \dfrac{\sqrt{5}-1}{2}$. Thus, $x = 1 + \langle x \rangle = \dfrac{1+\sqrt{5}}{2}$.

[**NOTE 1:** Of course, $x = 1.618$ is also acceptable!]

[**NOTE 2:** This value of x is called the *Golden Ratio*.]

Contests written and compiled by Steven R. Conrad & Daniel Flegler   Mathematics Leagues Inc., © 1993

Problem 5-1

Method I: Using a calculator, $A \approx 1.248963 \times 10^{23}$, and $B \approx 1.248967 \times 10^{23}$, so the larger one is $\boxed{B}$.

Method II: Here we'll show why an expression like A is *always* less than one like B. We know the value of
$A = (1993-3)(1993-2)(1993-1)(1993)(1993+1)(1993+2)(1993+3)$
$= (1993^2-9)(1993^2-4)(1993^2-1)(1993)$
$< (1993^2)(1993^2)(1993^2)(1993) = 1993^7 = B.$

Problem 5-2

To minimize the value of a, make the base get smaller as the exponent get larger. Therefore, the smallest possible value of a is $3^1 + 2^2 + 1^3 = \boxed{8}$.

Problem 5-3

Method I: Since the argument of $2\log_2(x-1)$ is $x-1$, this argument must be positive, so $x > 1$. So long as $x > 1$, $x+1 = (x-1)^2$. Solving, $x = 0$ or $x = 3$. We must reject $x = 0$, so the solution is $x = \boxed{3}$.

Method II: By the change of base theorem, we know
$\log_2(x+1) = \dfrac{\log(x+1)}{\log 2}$ and $2\log_2(x-1) = \dfrac{2\log(x-1)}{\log 2}$.
Changing *both* bases, the graphs of the resulting functions will intersect at the same point(s) as the graphs of the original functions. Changing the base to 10 (or to e) and using a graphing calculator, the solution can be found to the desired degree of accuracy.

Problem 5-4

Since $23! = 1\times2\times3\times4\times5\times \ldots \times22\times23$, we can drop the factor "1," so 23! equals the product of the **22** consecutive integers $2\times3\times4\times5\times \ldots \times22\times23$. Also, we can replace $2\times3\times4$ with the factor 24, so

$23! = 5\times \ldots \times23\times24$, a product of **20** consecutive integers. Thus, the other values of n are $\boxed{20, 22}$.

Problem 5-5

By rationalizing the denominator of the left side, we get $\dfrac{21+x+21-x+2\sqrt{21^2-x^2}}{21+x-21+x}$, or $\dfrac{21+\sqrt{21^2-x^2}}{x}$. This will equal $\dfrac{21}{x}$ if and only if $\sqrt{21^2-x^2} = 0$. The two solutions, both of which check, are $x = \boxed{21, -21}$.

Problem 5-6

In a triangle, the sum of any two sides is greater than the third side. Since $2x + 7 > 5x$, $x < \frac{7}{3}$. But $2x + 5x > 7$, so $x > 1$. Combining these conditions, $1 < x < \frac{7}{3}$.

Method I: The perimeter of the triangle is $7x+7$, so $14 < 7x+7 < 23\frac{1}{3}$. From the right side of this inequality, the largest integer which could be the perimeter of this triangle is $\boxed{23}$.

Method II: The perimeter of the triangle is $7x+7$. Since 7 is a prime, the perimeter will be integral if and only if x is a rational number with a denominator of 7. Since $x < \frac{7}{3}$, the largest such value of x is $\frac{16}{7}$, and the resulting perimeter is $7\left(\frac{16}{7}\right) + 7 = 23$.

Contests written and compiled by Steven R. Conrad & Daniel Flegler   Mathematics Leagues Inc., © 1993

Problem 6-1

When $x^2 = y^2$, either $x = y$ or $x = -y$. Since $x \neq y$, $x = -y$ and $x^3 + y^3 = x^3 + (-x)^3 = x^3 - x^3 = \boxed{0}$.

Problem 6-2

As shown in the diagram at the right, draw segments connecting both endpoints of one chord to the same endpoint of the other chord. This forms the right triangle shown with legs 10 and 24 and with hypotenuse $\boxed{26}$.

Problem 6-3

Change each base to a 2, so the equation becomes $(2^{4\sin^2 x})(2^{4\sin x})(2^1) = 2^{4\sin^2 x + 4\sin x + 1} = 2^0$. By equating exponents, we get $4\sin^2 x + 4\sin x + 1 = (2\sin x + 1)^2 = 0$. The least positive degree-measure of x for which $\sin x = -\frac{1}{2}$ is $\boxed{210°}$.

[**NOTE:** When $y = (16^{\sin^2 x})(4^{2\sin x})(2)$ and $y = 1$ are graphed on the same set of axes on a graphing calculator, the solution, 3.665, is in radians. To convert to degrees, you must multiply 3.665 by $\frac{180}{\pi}$.]

Problem 6-4

Since $0 < x < 1$, we know that $\frac{1993}{x} > 1993$. The least integer greater than 1993 is $\boxed{1994}$.

[**NOTE:** When $x = \frac{1993}{1994}$, then $\frac{1993}{x} = 1994$.]

Problem 6-5

Method I: The number of 4-digit numbers that *don't* contain a "1" is $9 \times 9 \times 9 \times 9$. This includes 0000, so the number of positive integers less than 10 000 that don't contain a "1" is $9^4 - 1 = 6560$. There are 9999 positive integers less than 10 000. The number that *do* contain one or more "1" is $9999 - 6560 = \boxed{3439}$.

Method II: There are $1 \times 10 \times 10 \times 10 = 1000$ numbers whose first "1" is in the thousands' place. There are $9 \times 1 \times 10 \times 10 = 900$ numbers whose first "1" is in the hundreds' place. There are $9 \times 9 \times 1 \times 10 = 810$ numbers whose first "1" in the tens' place. There are $9 \times 9 \times 9 \times 1 = 729$ numbers whose first "1" is in the units' place. Finally, $1000 + 900 + 810 + 729 = 3439$.

Problem 6-6

Method I: Since $64^{x+y} = 4\sqrt{2} \Leftrightarrow 2^{6(x+y)} = 2^{5/2}$, $x+y = \frac{5}{12}$. Since $64^{2x} + 64^{2y} = 12$, $2^{12x} + 2^{12y} = 12$. Substituting, $2^{12x} + 2^{5-12x} = 12$, or $2^{12x} + \frac{2^5}{2^{12x}} = 12$. If we let $2^{12x} = t$, then $t + \frac{32}{t} = 12$. Clearing fractions and rearranging, $t^2 - 12t + 32 = (t-8)(t-4) = 0$. Using $t = 8$ makes $x > y$. If $t = 8$, then $2^{12x} = 2^3$, so $x = \frac{1}{4}$. Finally, $x+y = \frac{5}{12}$, so $(x,y) = \boxed{\left(\frac{1}{4}, \frac{1}{6}\right)}$.

Method II: Letting $64^x = a$ and $64^y = b$, the original equations become $a^2 + b^2 = 12$ and $ab = 4\sqrt{2}$, from which we see that $a^2 + 2ab + b^2 = 12 + 8\sqrt{2}$. Simplifying, $(a+b)^2 = 12 + 8\sqrt{2}$. Since $a > 0$ and $b > 0$, $a+b = \sqrt{12 + 8\sqrt{2}} = \sqrt{12 + 2\sqrt{32}} = \sqrt{(\sqrt{4} + \sqrt{8})^2} = \sqrt{(2 + 2\sqrt{2})^2} = 2 + 2\sqrt{2}$. Therefore, $a+b = 2 + 2\sqrt{2}$ and $ab = 4\sqrt{2}$. Since $x > y$, $a = 2\sqrt{2}$ and $b = 2$. Substituting into the two equations at the start of this solution, $64^x = 2^{6x} = 2^{3/2}$. Solving, $6x = \frac{3}{2}$ and $x = \frac{1}{4}$. Also, $64^y = 2^{6y} = 2$, so $6y = 1$, $y = \frac{1}{6}$, and $(x,y) = \left(\frac{1}{4}, \frac{1}{6}\right)$.

Contests written and compiled by Steven R. Conrad & Daniel Flegler   Mathematics Leagues Inc., © 1993

Problem 1

The product is 140, so let's factor: $140 = 2 \times 2 \times 5 \times 7$. The only arrangement of factors into an increasing sequence of one-digit numbers is $4 \times 5 \times 7$, so my street address is $\boxed{457}$.

Problem 2

The roots are integers, so the left side factors. Since there's only one positive value of a, 1993 must be prime. Factoring, $(x + 1993)(x + 1) = 0$. Multiplying, $x^2 + 1994x + 1993 = 0$, so $a = \boxed{1994}$.

Problem 3

Method I: In the diagram, there's a rt. $\triangle$ with hypotenuse $\overline{AB}$ and legs 8 and $(1+2+4+8)$ $= 15$. By the Pythagorean Theorem, $AB = \boxed{17}$.

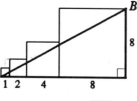

Method II: Coordinatize. Using $A(0,0)$ and $B(15,8)$, we can use the distance formula to get $AB = 17$.

[**NOTE:** The upper-left hand vertices of these squares are collinear, as are the upper right-hand vertices.]

Problem 4

Make a list: $1^3 = 1$; $2^3 = 8$; $3^3 = 27$; $4^3 = 64$; $5^3 = 125$; and $6^3 = 216$. Differences between cubes get ever larger, so no two can differ by 64, and the answer is $\boxed{0}$.

[**NOTE:** In 1637, French lawyer and provincial supreme court justice Pierre de Fermat, whose hobby and passion was mathematics, claimed that $a^n + b^n = c^n$, $n \geq 3$, is unsolvable in positive integers. [For $n = 2$, the solutions are known as *Pythagorean triples*.] Though Fermat (whose invention of analytic geometry is often erroneously credited to Déscartes) claimed he had found a truly wonderful proof, he said the margin of the book in which he wrote what came to be known as *Fermat's Last Theorem* was too narrow for the proof. He died 11 years later without offering his proof. The search for a proof, which became the most famous mathematics problem in history, ended when Andrew Wiles, of Princeton University, published his proof in the Spring of 1995.]

Problem 5

To maximize the triangle's area, let 60 be the length of the *shortest* altitude. The shortest altitude is drawn to the longest side, the hypotenuse. Since $(60)(5k) = (3k)(4k)$, $k = 25$. The area of the triangle is $150k = 150(25) = \boxed{3750}$.

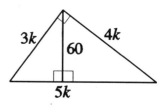

Problem 6

Method I: For each subset S that contains any given number, there's a subset S', called *the complement of* S, that does not contain that number; so each number appears in just half the subsets. Since each number occurs $\frac{1}{2} \times 256 = 128$ times, the required sum is $128 \times (1+2+ \ldots +8) = \boxed{4608}$.

Method II: The subset with all 8 numbers as elements has an element sum of $1+2+ \ldots +8 = 36$, so the average subset has an element sum half as great, 18. Finally, $256 \times 18 = 4608$.

Method III: On average, there are 4 elements per subset; and the average value of an element is $4\frac{1}{2}$. The average sum $= 4 \times 4\frac{1}{2} = 18$, and $256 \times 18 = 4608$.

Method IV: Each number appears in just half the subsets (see Method I). The total of the sums equals the total of the sums of 128 sets, each containing all the numbers; and $128 \times (1+2+ \ldots +8) = 4608$.

Contests written and compiled by Steven R. Conrad & Daniel Flegler   Mathematics Leagues Inc., © 1993

Problem 2-1

If $x + y = x - y$, then $y = 0$, so $xy = \boxed{0}$.

Problem 2-2

Call the prime p. The only possible factors are 1, -1, p, and $-p$. The product is p, so factors are $-p$, -1, and 1. Finally, since $1 - (-1) = -1 - (-p)$, $p = 3$. In any order, the answers are $\boxed{-3, -1, 1}$.

Problem 2-3

Since $\angle CAT$ intercepts $\frac{17}{20}$ of the circle, and $\angle DOG$ intercepts $\frac{3}{20}$ of the circle, the sum of their degree-measures will be equal to $\frac{1}{2}\left(\frac{17}{20} + \frac{3}{20}\right)(360) = \boxed{180}$.

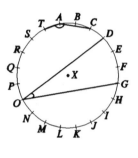

[**NOTE:** $m\angle CAT + m\angle DOG = 5\,m\angle PET$. We encourage you to send us similar "stupid pet tricks."]

Problem 2-4

Method I: Any number divisible by 45 is divisible by 5. To be divisible by 5, the final digit must be 0 or 5. The only such 5-digit numbers are 19930 and 19935. By calculator, the only one divisible by 45 is $\boxed{19935}$.

Method II: For an integer to be divisible by 9, the sum of its digits must be divisible by 9. The sum of the digits of 19935 is 27, so 19935 is the smallest 5-digit number divisible by 9. Since 19935 is also divisible by 5, 19935 is divisible by $9 \times 5 = 45$.

Problem 2-5

Let $CF = x$. Since the diameter of the circle is 20, $AF = 20-x$. Tangents to a circle from the same outside point are congruent, so $AD = AF = 20 - x$, and $CE = CF = x$. Since the perimeter of $\triangle ABC$ is 42, $EB + BD + AD + AF + CF + CE = EB + BD + 40 = 42$, and $EB + BD = \boxed{2}$.

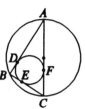

Problem 2-6

We'd like to rewrite the first equation as $(c^a)^{1/a} = (b^{2a})^{1/a}$; but we can't if $a = 0$. There are two cases: if $a = 0$, then, from the second equation, $c = 1$, and, from the third equation, $b = 9$; but if $a \neq 0$, then $c = b^2$ (and, if a is even, it is also possible that $c = -b^2$). From the second equation, $2^c = 2(4^a) = 2(2^2)^a = 2^{2a+1}$, so $c = 2a+1$. Substituting $a = \frac{1}{2}(c-1)$, and then $c = -b^2$, into the third equation, we get $3b^2 - 2b + 21 = 0$ (which has no real roots). But if we substitute $a = \frac{1}{2}(c-1)$, and then $c = b^2$, we get $3b^2 + 2b - 21 = (3b-7)(b+3) = 0$; so $b = -3$ or $-\frac{7}{3}$. The solutions are: $\boxed{(0,9,1),\ (4,-3,9),\ \left(\frac{20}{9}, \frac{7}{3}, \frac{49}{9}\right)}$.

Contests written and compiled by Steven R. Conrad & Daniel Flegler   **Mathematics Leagues Inc.,** © 1993

Problem 3-1

Method I: The problem implies that, *whichever number we use as the first odd integer*, the value $B - A$ is fixed; so let's calculate a specific sum. On a calculator, if $A = 1 + 3 + \ldots + 19 = 100$, then, for this value of A, $21 + \ldots + 39 = 300 = B$, and $B - A = \boxed{200}$.

Method II: Each number in the second set is 20 more than the corresponding number in the first set. Since there are 10 numbers in the second set, their excess over the first set is $20 \times 10 = 200$.

Problem 3-2

$1994x^2 + x - 1993 = (x + 1)(1994x - 1993) = 0$, so $x = \boxed{-1, \dfrac{1993}{1994}}$.

Problem 3-3

Method I: Let the lengths of the sides of the unshaded squares be x and $x+8$. Since $x^2 + (x+8)^2 = 1000$, we get $x^2 + 8x - 468 = (x - 18)(x + 26)$

$= 0$. Using $x = 18$, the area of each shaded rectangle is $x(x+8) = 468$, so the required area is $\boxed{936}$.

Method II: As in Method I, $x^2 + (x+8)^2 = 1000$, or $2x^2 + 16x = 936$. But, we don't need the value of x. All we need is $2(x)(x+8) = 2x^2 + 16x = 936$.

Method III: Let the lengths of the sides of the unshaded squares be $x-4$ and $x+4$. If we expand and simplify $(x-4)^2 + (x+4)^2 = 1000$, we will get $x^2 = 484$, so $2(x-4)(x+4) = 2(x^2 - 16) = 2(484 - 16) = 936$.

Problem 3-4

Method I: On my first 4 flips, there are $2^4 = 16$ possible outcomes. Of these, there are 4 ways to get 3 heads and 1 tail and 1 way to get 4 heads. Since 5 of the 16 possible outcomes are favorable, the probability is $\boxed{\dfrac{5}{16}}$.

Method II: There are 4 favorable cases: start with 3 heads in a row, *HHH*, which has a probability of $\frac{1}{8}$, or have 3 *H*'s and 1 *T* in the first 4 throws, without starting with 3 *H*'s in a row: *THHH, HTHH, HHTH*, each with probability of $\frac{1}{16}$. Now add: $\frac{1}{8} + \frac{3}{16} = \frac{5}{16}$.

Method III: This an example of a set of *Bernoulli Trials* in which we seek the probability that there are at least 3 heads in 4 trials. The required probability is $\binom{4}{3}\left(\frac{1}{2}\right)^3\left(\frac{1}{2}\right)^1 + \binom{4}{4}\left(\frac{1}{2}\right)^4\left(\frac{1}{2}\right)^0 = \frac{5}{16}$.

Problem 3-5

From the first equation, $x = \frac{7}{3}y$. Substituting into the second equation, $y^7 = x^3 = \left(\frac{7}{3}y\right)^3$. Let's solve for y. If $y = 0$, then $x = 0$. If $y \neq 0$, then $y^4 = \left(\frac{7}{3}\right)^3$, so the positive value of y is $\left(\frac{7}{3}\right)^{\frac{3}{4}}$. Since $x = \frac{7}{3}y$, $x = \left(\frac{7}{3}\right)^{\frac{7}{4}}$. The two solutions are $\boxed{(0,0), \left(\left(\frac{7}{3}\right)^{\frac{7}{4}}, \left(\frac{7}{3}\right)^{\frac{3}{4}}\right)}$.

[**NOTE:** Alternatively, one can graphically locate the first quadrant intersection of $y = \frac{3}{7}x$ and $y = x^{\frac{3}{7}}$.]

Problem 3-6

Let a_n = my investment's \$ value at the end of the nth day. Then $a_{n+1} = a_n + \frac{p}{100}a_n - \frac{n+1}{4}\frac{p}{100}a_n$
$$= \left(1 + \frac{p}{100}\left(1 - \frac{n+1}{4}\right)\right)a_n.$$
Since $a_{1000} = 0$, let $n+1 = 1000$ to get the equation $0 = \left(1 + \frac{p}{100}\left(1 - \frac{1000}{4}\right)\right)a_{999}$. Since $a_{999} \neq 0$, we get $1 + \frac{p}{100}\left(1 - \frac{1000}{4}\right) = 0$. Solving, $p = \boxed{\dfrac{100}{249}}$.

[**NOTE:** This type of relationship is called a *recursion*, and the functions involved are called *recursive functions*.]

Contests written and compiled by Steven R. Conrad & Daniel Flegler   **Mathematics Leagues Inc.,** © 1994

Problem 4-1

Unless every * is the digit 9, the sum will not exceed 389. If each * is the digit 9, then the sum is 390, and ☼ = $\boxed{0}$.

```
  * 3
  * *
  * *
  * *
 ────
 3 9 ☼
```

Problem 4-2

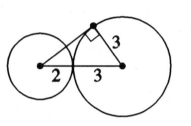

Since a tangent is perpendicular to a radius drawn to the point of contact, the triangle shown is a right triangle whose hypotenuse is $2+3 = 5$. Since the leg shown is 3, the other leg is $\boxed{4}$.

Problem 4-3

Expressions like these have "towers" of exponents. Since exponential towers are computed from the top down, not from the bottom up, $2^{3^5} = 2^{243}$, $2^{5^3} = 2^{125}$, $3^{2^5} = 3^{32}$, $3^{5^2} = 3^{25}$, $5^{2^3} = 5^8$, and $5^{3^2} = 5^9$. Of these, the largest is the first, $\boxed{2^{3^5}}$.

Problem 4-4

It took the car 4 minutes, and the runner 20 minutes to get to where the car stopped. The additional number of minutes it took the runner was $20-4 = \boxed{16}$.

Problem 4-5

Let the numbers be x and $3x$. If x is smaller, then $4x = 8+2x$, and $x = 4$. But, if $3x$ is smaller, then $4x = 8+6x$, $x = -4$, and $3x = \boxed{-12}$.

Problem 4-6

Clearly, if we choose the 997 even numbers (or if we choose the numbers 998, 999, . . . , 1994), the sum is never 1995. Let's show that 997 is the greatest *possible* value of N: Write the members of the original sequence as 1, 2, 3, . . . , 996, 997, (1995−997), (1995−996), (1995−995), . . . , (1995−1). Now, if both x and 1995−x are chosen, the sum will be 1995. But, if we choose more than 997 numbers (that is, more than half the numbers), we *must* have one such pair. Consequently, the greatest *possible* value is $\boxed{997}$.

[**NOTE:** The mathematical basis for the above solution is known as the *Pigeonhole Principle*.]

Contests written and compiled by Steven R. Conrad & Daniel Flegler   Mathematics Leagues Inc., © 1994

Problem 5-1

Subtracting the second equation from the first, $c + d = -1$, so $1994(c+d) = 1994(-1) = \boxed{-1994}$.

Problem 5-2

Since the length of the altitude to the base is 20, the area of the triangle is 300. This altitude splits the original triangle into two 15–20–25 right triangles. Let h be the length of an altitude to one of the legs. Since $25h = 600$, $h = \boxed{24}$.

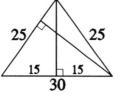

[**NOTE:** The altitude to the leg splits the original triangle into two right triangles: 7–24–25 and 18–24–30.]

Problem 5-3

Method I: Draw $\overline{AC}$. Since the slopes of $\overline{AO}$ and $\overline{AC}$ are negative reciprocals, $\overline{AO}$ and $\overline{AC}$ are perpendicular. Since $AO = AC$, $\triangle AOC$ is also isosceles, so $m\angle AOC = \boxed{45 \text{ or } 45°}$.

Method II: In the first diagram, compute the lengths $AO = \sqrt{10}$, $AC = \sqrt{10}$, and $OC = \sqrt{20}$, making $\triangle AOC$ an isosceles right triangle.

Method III: Draw $\overline{AD}$. Since $\overline{AD} \perp \overline{OD}$ and $\overline{AD} \cong \overline{OD}$, $\triangle ADO$ is an isosceles right triangle, and $m\angle AOC = 45$.

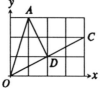

Problem 5-4

Method I: The conjunction $2x \leq y \leq 5x \Leftrightarrow 2x \leq y$ and $y \leq 5x \Leftrightarrow \frac{y}{5} \leq x$ and $x \leq \frac{y}{2}$. Hence $\frac{y}{5} \leq x \leq \frac{y}{2}$, and (a,b) is equal to $\boxed{\left(\frac{1}{5}, \frac{1}{2}\right)}$.

Method II: From the given inequalities, if x is negative, then y is negative; and if y is negative, then x is negative. If $xy \neq 0$, then taking reciprocals reverses the inequality, so $\frac{1}{2x} \geq \frac{1}{y} \geq \frac{1}{5x}$. Multiplying by the positive number xy, we get $\frac{y}{2} \geq x \geq \frac{y}{5}$, so $\frac{y}{5} \leq x \leq \frac{y}{2}$, an inequality which is also satisfied by $(x,y) = (0,0)$.

Problem 5-5

Let the greatest common factor of the two integers be g. Then, for some integer k, the smaller of the two integers is kg, and the larger is $kg + g = (k+1)g$. Their product is $k(k+1)g^2 = 9984 = 12 \times 13 \times 8^2$, so the integers are 12×8 and 13×8, or $\boxed{96, 104}$.

Problem 5-6

Method I: Expanding $(\log 3 + \log x)(\log 5 + \log x) = k$,

$*$ $(\log x)^2 + (\log 15)(\log x) + (\text{other terms}) = 0$.

For $x^2 + bx + c = 0$ to have but one root, the equation must have the form $(x + \frac{1}{2}b)^2 = 0$. Thus, $*$ has the form $(\log x + \frac{1}{2}\log 15)^2 = 0$, and $\log x = -\frac{1}{2}\log 15$. Finally, $x = \boxed{\frac{1}{\sqrt{15}}}$.

Method II: A quadratic equation has only one root if its discriminant is 0, so $(\log 15)^2 - 4(\log 3 \log 5 - k) = 0$, and $k = \log 3 \log 5 - \frac{1}{4}(\log 15)^2$. Substitute this value for k in $(\log x)^2 + \log 15 \log x + \log 3 \log 5 - k = 0$, solve for $\log x$ by factoring or the quadratic formula, then obtain x by using the relation $x = 10^{\log x}$.

Contests written and compiled by Steven R. Conrad & Daniel Flegler   **Mathematics Leagues Inc., © 1994**

Problem 6-1

Mehtod I: To go from one term to the next, you add 4. If you do this 61 times, you'll add $61 \times 4 = 244$ to 7, and you'll get $7 + 244 = \boxed{251 \text{ or } \$2.51}$.

Method II: Notice that the sequence includes both 7 and 27. It also includes $47, 67, 87, \ldots, 247$. Now, add 4 to get to the next term, 251.

Method III: The nth term of the sequence is $4n+3$. When $n = 62$, the term is $4 \times 62 + 3 = 251$.

Problem 6-2

Factoring, $x(x-1)(x+1) = 1994(x-1)(x+1)$, so the three values of x are $\boxed{-1, 1, 1994}$.

Problem 6-3

Since $m\angle OAC > m\angle OBC$, it follows that $CA < CB$. Next, O is in the plane, and $\overline{CO} \perp$ plane, so $\triangle AOC$ and $\triangle BOC$ are right triangles. Thus, $CO = \frac{AC}{\sqrt{2}} = \frac{\sqrt{3}}{\sqrt{2}}$, and $BC = 2CO = \frac{2\sqrt{3}}{\sqrt{2}}$. Now, $AB = \sqrt{AC^2 + BC^2} = \sqrt{3+6} = \boxed{3}$.

Problem 6-4

Since x, y, and z are consecutive integers, $z = y+1$ and $x = y-1$. Since $z^2 - x^2 = 888$, $(y+1)^2 - (y-1)^2 = 888$. Solving, $y = \boxed{222}$.

Problem 6-5

The central angle opposite the shortest side must be less than or equal to $\frac{360°}{12} = 30°$. The larger this angle is, the longer the shortest side is, so the length sought is maximized when the polygon is regular.

Method I (Basic Trigonometry): Draw an apothem to one side of the regular 12-sided polygon. Using right triangle trigonometry in either 15°-90°-75° triangle thus formed, $\frac{x}{2} = \sin 15°$, so $x = \boxed{2 \sin 15°}$.

Method II (Trigonometry): Using the law of cosines, $x^2 = 1^2 + 1^2 - 2(1)(1)(\cos 30°)$. Solving for x, we get $x = \boxed{\sqrt{2 - \sqrt{3}}}$.

[**NOTE:** $\sqrt{2 - \sqrt{3}} = \frac{\sqrt{6} - \sqrt{2}}{2} = 2 \sin 15° \approx 0.517638 \ldots$]

Method III (Geometry): Drop an altitude to one of the legs. As in the diagram, we get a 30°-60°-90° triangle and another right triangle. Using the Pythagorean Theorem in this other triangle, $x^2 = \left(\frac{1}{2}\right)^2 + \left(1 - \frac{\sqrt{3}}{2}\right)^2 = 2 - \sqrt{3}$. Now take the square root to get the value of x.

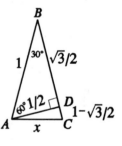

Problem 6-6

Notice that, as x increases, $f(x)$ decreases, so f is a decreasing function, and $f(a) > f(b) \Leftrightarrow a < b$. The given inequality is of the form $f(f(x)) > f(1-5x)$. By the first sentence, this implies that $f(x) < 1 - 5x$, or $1 - x - x^3 < 1 - 5x \Leftrightarrow x^3 - 4x = x(x + 2)(x - 2) > 0$. Thus, $\boxed{-2 < x < 0 \text{ or } x > 2. \textit{(Both required.)}}$

Contests written and compiled by Steven R. Conrad & Daniel Flegler   Mathematics Leagues Inc., © 1994

Problem 1-1

The sum of the two primes is 999, so one of them must be the even number 2, the other must be the odd number 997. Their product is $2 \times 997 = \boxed{1994}$.

Problem 1-2

Method I: A person born in 1940 was 40 years old in 1980, since $1940 + 40 = 1980$. Note that the person's age then, 40, was half the last two digits of the year (since half of 80 is 40). Using this idea, my grandmother's age in 1950 was half of 50, which is 25 (since $1925 + 25 = 1950$) and the age of her grandmother (who was born in the previous century) was half of $150 = 75$, since $1875 + 75 = 1950$. So, in 1950, my grandmother was 25 and her grandmother was $\boxed{75}$.

Method II: Let my grandmother's grandmother's age in 1950 be x. Then $1950 - x = 1800 + x$ (the 19th century year in which my grandmother's grandmother was born), so $x = 75$.

Problem 1-3

Let n be the number of times that 17^2 appears in the radicand. Then $\sqrt{17^2 n} = 17^2$. Squaring both sides, we get $17^2 n = 17^4$. Dividing both sides by 17^2, we find that $n = \boxed{17^2}$.

Problem 1-4

As can be seen at the right, the distance between the centers is the length of the hypotenuse of an isosceles right triangle with legs of 7. The answer is $\boxed{7\sqrt{2}}$.

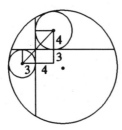

Problem 1-5

Method I: $1 \div 49 = 0.020408163\mathbf{265}306\ldots$ is obtainable by hand (if not on a 10-digit calculator), so $x = \boxed{65}$.

Method II: It sure *seems* that $\frac{1}{49} = \sum_{n=1}^{\infty} \frac{2^n}{10^{2n}} = \sum_{n=1}^{\infty} \frac{1}{50^n}$ (which is easily verified by using the formula for the sum of an *infinite* geometric series). Since our series is not infinite, let's write out several terms of the infinite series to see what's happening:

$$\frac{1}{49} = \ldots + \frac{32}{10^{10}} + \frac{64}{10^{12}} + \frac{128}{10^{14}} + \text{smaller terms}$$
$$= \ldots + \frac{32}{10^{10}} + \frac{64}{10^{12}} + \frac{100}{10^{14}} + \frac{28}{10^{14}} + \ldots$$
$$= \ldots + \frac{32}{10^{10}} + \frac{64}{10^{12}} + \frac{1}{10^{12}} + \frac{28}{10^{14}} + \ldots$$
$$= \ldots + \frac{32}{10^{10}} + \frac{65}{10^{12}} + \frac{28}{10^{14}} + \frac{256}{10^{16}} + \ldots.$$

From the line above, to the nearest integer, $x = 65$.

Method III: By calculator, *solve for x* (!!!!) by first subtracting the first five terms on the right from $1/49$, then multiplying the result by 10^{12} to obtain 65.31.

Problem 1-6

Method I: Let $a = \frac{3x+25}{2x-5}$. Then, $2a = \frac{6x+50}{2x-5}$. By long division, $2a = 3 + \frac{65}{2x-5}$. Now, only if $\frac{65}{2x-5}$ is odd will $2a$ be even and will a be integral. Therefore, $2x-5$ must be a divisor of 65 with an odd quotient. There are 8 possibilities: If $2x-5 = \pm 1, \pm 5, \pm 13, \pm 65$, then, respectively, $2x = 5 \pm 1, 5 \pm 5, 5 \pm 13, 5 \pm 65$. The sum of these values of $2x$ is $8 \times 5 = 40$; and the sum of the values of x is half as much, $\boxed{20}$.

Method II: On a graphing calculator, let

$$y_1 = \frac{3x+25}{2x-5}.$$

Now, under the **ZOOM** menu, select **INTEGER**. Next, when you **GRAPH** and then **TRACE**, you'll see that the value of y is an integer only for the eight values of x listed above. If you have a **TABLE** feature on your calculator, use **TBL SET** to set the difference between consecutive x-values as 1 (*i.e.*, make Δtbl = 1). Then, quickly scan the table for integer values of y. You'll find them only at the eight x-values listed above.

Contests written and compiled by Steven R. Conrad & Daniel Flegler   **Mathematics Leagues Inc.,** © 1994

Problem 2-1

If $xy = \frac{1}{x} \cdot \frac{1}{y} = \frac{1}{xy}$, then $(xy)^2 = 1$ and $xy = \boxed{\pm 1}$.

Problem 2-2

Method I: Since $AF = 5$ and $AB = 4$, if follows that $BF = 3$. Since $BC = 4$ and $BF = 3$, $CF = 1$. Similarly, $BE = 1$. Finally, $EF = BC - BE - CF = 4 - 1 - 1 = \boxed{2}$.

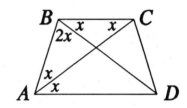

Method II: Since $AF = 5$ and $AB = 4$, if follows that $BF = 3$. Similarly, $CE = 3$. Since $BC = 4$ and $BF + CE = 3 + 3 = 6$, we see that $EF = 6 - 4 = 2$.

Problem 2-3

Since 100 and 164 differ by 64, the question boils down to this: Is there any pair of integers, both perfect squares and both less than $100 + 125 = 225$ and $164 + 125 = 289$, which differ by 64? There are *two* such pairs: 0 and 64, and 36 and 100. These solutions correspond, respectively, to $n = -100$ and $n = -64$, so the one who was right was $\boxed{\text{Prof. Clever}}$.

Problem 2-4

The sum of the roots of $ax^2 + bx + c = 0$ is $-\frac{b}{a}$, so $r + s = 26$ and $19r + 94s = 1994$. Multiply the first equation by -19 and add it to the second equation to get $s = 20$, then $r = 6$, then $c = rs = \boxed{120}$.

Problem 2-5

Method I: The graph of $y = \big| 2 - |1 - |x|| \big|$, sketched at the right, crosses the line $y = 1$ at $x = \boxed{\pm 4, \pm 2, 0}$.

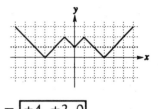

Method II: $\big| 2 - |1 - |x|| \big| = 1 \Longleftrightarrow \big| ||x| - 1| - 2 \big| = 1$, so $||x| - 1| - 2 = \pm 1$ and $||x| - 1| = 3$ or 1. Next, $|x| - 1 = \pm 3$ or ± 1. Consequently, $|x| = 4$, -2, 2, or 0 and $x = \pm 4, \pm 2, 0$.

Problem 2-6

$\triangle ABD \cong \triangle DCA$, so the altitude from B to $\overline{AD}$ is congruent to the altitude from C to $\overline{AD}$; and $ABCD$ is an isosceles trapezoid. Since $\overline{BC} \parallel \overline{AD}$, it follows that $\angle BCA \cong \angle CAD$. Since $\triangle ABC$ is isosceles, $\angle BAC \cong \angle BCA$. Since $\triangle ADB$ is isosceles, $\angle BAD \cong \angle DBA$. Now, in $\triangle ABC$, $5x = 180$; so $x = 36$ and $m\angle ABC = 3x = 3(36) = \boxed{108}$.

Contests written and compiled by Steven R. Conrad & Daniel Flegler   Mathematics Leagues Inc., © 1994

Problem 3-1

Let the price, *after* reduction, be x times the original price. Then, $25x$ is the price after the first reduction; and the price after two reductions is $25x^2 = 16$. Continuing, $x^2 = \frac{16}{25}$, so $x = \frac{4}{5} = 80\%$, and the percent price reduction each time was $\boxed{20 \text{ or } 20\%}$.

Problem 3-2

In any circle with a chord of length 8, it is always possible to draw a second chord, perpendicular to the first, whose length is *any* positive number less than 8. Therefore, we seek the smallest circle in which it is possible to have a chord of length 8. This circle has a diameter of length 8 and an area of $\boxed{16\pi}$.

Problem 3-3

For the moment, let's see if we can create a six-term increasing arithmetic sequence whose first term is 100 and whose sixth term is 200. With a first term of 100, the total amount by which we must increase is $200 - 100 = 100$. Since the increase occurs in five equally spaced intervals, the difference between successive terms is 20. Finally, if we change the 170 to 180, the additional number we'd still need is $\boxed{120}$.

Problem 3-4

Method I: Factoring further, $1995 = 3 \times 5 \times 7 \times 19$. To write 1995 as a product of three factors, each larger than 1, we must pair two of the four prime factors. The number of ways we can do this is $\binom{4}{2} = \boxed{6}$.

Method II: The smallest factor, x, can be 3, 5, or 7. Let's find all triples (x,y,z), with $1 < x < y < z$, for each value of x. If $x = 3$, we have $(3,5,7\times19)$, $(3,7,5\times19)$, or $(3,19,5\times7)$; if $x = 5$, we have $(5,7,3\times19)$ or $(5,19,3\times7)$; and if $x = 7$, we have $(7,3\times5,19)$. The total number of triples is 6.

Problem 3-5

An expression of the form y^a will equal 1 in only three circumstances: 1) when $a = 0$; 2) when $y = 1$; and 3) when $y = -1$ and a is an even number. Let's consider each case:

Case 1: If $x^2 - 7x + 12 = (x-3)(x-4) = 0$, then $x = 3$ (and $y = 3$) or $x = 4$ (and $y = 2$).

Case 2: If $y = 1$, then $x = 5$.

Case 3: If $y = -1$, then $x = 7$ and $x^2 - 7x + 12 = 12$, an even number.

Altogether, the solutions are the four ordered pairs $\boxed{(3,3),\ (4,2),\ (5,1),\ (7,-1)}$.

Problem 3-6

The shaded triangles are similar. Since the ratio of their areas is $\frac{32}{18} = \frac{16}{9}$, the

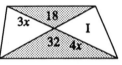

ratio of the lengths of corrsponding sides is $\sqrt{\frac{16}{9}} = \frac{4}{3}$, as shown in the diagram. Since $\triangle I$ and the smaller shaded triangle have the same altitude (from the trapezoid's upper right vertex) and their bases are in the ratio 4:3, the area of $\triangle I = \frac{4}{3} \times 18 = 24$. Finally, $18 + 32 + 24 + 24 = \boxed{98}$.

[NOTE: Since a similar argument applies to either unshaded triangle, their areas are each 24. In any trapezoid, regardless of shape, the unshaded triangles will always have equal areas.]

Contests written and compiled by Steven R. Conrad & Daniel Flegler

Mathematics Leagues Inc., © 1995

Problem 4-1

There are two possibilities: the lengths of the legs could be 3 and 4 (making the length of the hypotenuse 5), or the length of one leg could be 3 and the length of the hypotenuse could be 4, making the length of the third side $= \sqrt{4^2 - 3^2} = \boxed{\sqrt{7}}$.

Problem 4-2

If $5^n + 5^n + 5^n + 5^n + 5^n = 5 \times 5^n = 5^{n+1} = 5^{25}$, then $n + 1 = 25$ and $n = \boxed{24}$.

Problem 4-3

The given vertices lie on one of the square's diagonals. Since the slope of this diagonal is $-\frac{3}{2}$, the slope of the other diagonal is $\frac{2}{3}$. The midpoint of both diagonals is (8,6). The other vertices are at $\boxed{(5,4),\ (11,8)}$.

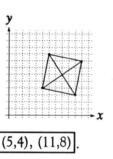

Problem 4-4

Method I: Since $(1+i)^2 = 2i$, we know $(1+i)^{13} = (2i)^6(1+i) = (64i^6)(1+i) = (-64)(1+i) = -64-64i$, so $(a,b) = \boxed{(-64,-64)}$.

Method II: By DeMoivre's Theorem, since $(1+i) = \sqrt{2}\operatorname{cis}45°$, we know that $(1+i)^{13} = (\sqrt{2})^{13}\operatorname{cis}585° = 64\sqrt{2}\operatorname{cis}225° = -64 + -64i = -64 - 64i$.

Problem 4-5

As can be seen in the diagram at the right, there are two equilateral triangles that can circumscribe this hexagon. The larger triangle has a side-length of 30, and the smaller one has a side-length of $\boxed{27}$.

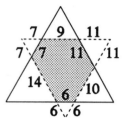

Problem 4-6

We have $a_{n+1} = \dfrac{a_n}{1+a_n}$. Hence, $\dfrac{1}{a_{n+1}} = \dfrac{1+a_n}{a_n}$, or $\dfrac{1}{a_{n+1}} = \dfrac{1}{a_n} + 1$. Let's use this recursion repeatedly and see what develops:

$$\frac{1}{a_1} = \frac{1}{1995}.$$
$$\frac{1}{a_2} = \frac{1}{a_1} + 1 = \frac{1}{1995} + 1.$$
$$\frac{1}{a_3} = \frac{1}{a_2} + 1 = \left(\frac{1}{a_1}+1\right)+1 = \frac{1}{a_1}+2 = \frac{1}{1995}+2.$$
$$\frac{1}{a_4} = \frac{1}{a_3} + 1 = \left(\frac{1}{a_1}+2\right)+1 = \frac{1}{a_1}+3 = \frac{1}{1995}+3.$$
$$\frac{1}{a_5} = \frac{1}{a_4} + 1 = \left(\frac{1}{a_1}+3\right)+1 = \frac{1}{a_1}+4 = \frac{1}{1995}+4.$$

By induction,

$$\frac{1}{a_{1995}} = \frac{1}{1995} + 1994 = \frac{1+1994\times1995}{1995} = \frac{3978031}{1995}.$$

Taking reciprocals,

$$a_{1995} = \boxed{\frac{1995}{3978031} \text{ or } 0.0005015}.$$

[**NOTE:** Since answers must be exact or must have 4 (or more) significant digits, correctly rounded, an answer of 0.0005 must **NOT** receive credit. The answer 0.0005 has only 1 significant digit, not the 4 (or more) that are required for an approximate answer to receive credit.]

Contests written and compiled by Steven R. Conrad & Daniel Flegler   Mathematics Leagues Inc., © 1995

Problem 5-1

The first n has at most nine digits. After the first application of the two-step process, the new n has three digits. The next n also has three digits and must exhibit one of four patterns: 303, 123, 213, or 033. At this point, the next iteration of any of these four patterns maps to the unique fixed image $\boxed{123}$.

Problem 5-2

The radius of the circle is the hypotenuse of an isosceles right triangle whose leg is 1. The area of the circle is $\boxed{2\pi}$.

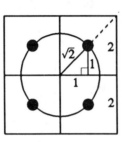

Problem 5-3

If the even number 270 is divided by an odd number, then the quotient, when integral, must be even. Since the only even prime is 2, $\frac{270}{x} = 2$ and $x = \boxed{135}$.

Problem 5-4

Method I: On a scientific calculator, start with any intitial guess x_0, and *keep pressing the cos key!* The sequence x_0, $\cos x_0$, $\cos(\cos x_0)$, . . . eventually settles down. One can verify that, to many significant digits, $\cos(0.739085133215\ldots) = \boxed{0.739085133215\ldots}$.

[**NOTE:** To four significant digits, the answer is 0.7391]

Method II: On a TI81 graphing calculator, let $y_1 = \cos x - x$. Using **GRAPH**, **TRACE**, and **ZOOM** the zero of this function is 0.7391, to four significant digits. On a TI82, **GRAPH** and use **CALC** to get this answer.

Problem 5-5

Method I: The probability that Pat wins on the first round is $\frac{1}{2}$. The probability that Lee wins on the first round is $\frac{1}{2} \times \frac{1}{6}$. The ratio of these probabilities is 6:1, with Pat favored. These statements hold any round, so the probability that Lee wins is $\frac{1}{6+1} = \boxed{\frac{1}{7}}$.

Method II: The probability that Lee wins on the first round is $\frac{1}{2} \times \frac{1}{6}$. Subsequently, the probability that Lee wins equals the probability that no one won on any previous round times the probability that Lee wins on *that* round. The result is the infinite geometric series $\frac{1}{2} \times \frac{1}{6} + (\frac{1}{2} \times \frac{5}{6})(\frac{1}{2} \times \frac{1}{6}) + (\frac{1}{2} \times \frac{5}{6})^2(\frac{1}{2} \times \frac{1}{6}) + \cdots$, in which $a_1 = \frac{1}{12}$ and $r = \frac{5}{12}$. This series' sum is $\frac{1}{7}$.

Problem 5-6

Rewrite the equations, this time using fractional exponents, to get $x^2 + x \cdot x^{\frac{1}{3}} \cdot y^{\frac{2}{3}} = x^{\frac{4}{3}}(x^{\frac{2}{3}} + y^{\frac{2}{3}}) = 208$ and $y^2 + y \cdot y^{\frac{1}{3}} \cdot x^{\frac{2}{3}} = y^{\frac{4}{3}}(y^{\frac{2}{3}} + x^{\frac{2}{3}}) = 1053$.

These two equations have a common factor. Since x and y are both clearly non-zero, we can divide the new first equation by the new second equation to get $\left(\frac{x}{y}\right)^{\frac{4}{3}} = \frac{208}{1053} = \frac{16 \times 13}{81 \times 13} = \frac{16}{81}$. Since $\frac{x}{y} = \pm\frac{8}{27}$, we get $y = \pm\frac{27x}{8}$. The first equation becomes $x^2 + \frac{9}{4}x^2 = 208$. Solving, $x^2 = 64$ and $x = \pm 8$. Finally, $y = \pm 27$, and $(x,y) = \boxed{(8,27),\ (8,-27),\ (-8,27),\ (-8,-27)}$.

[**NOTE:** The substitution $y = kx$, used together with the techniques shown above, also yields a solution.]

Contests written and compiled by Steven R. Conrad & Daniel Flegler   Mathematics Leagues Inc., © 1995

Problem 6-1

Squaring both sides, $\sqrt{n} = n$. Squaring again, $n = n^2$. The two solutions, both of which check in the original equation, are $\boxed{0, 1}$.

Problem 6-2

Method I: Using the diagram at the right, it is easy to see that the perimeter of the smaller equilateral triangle is $\boxed{3\sqrt{3}}$.

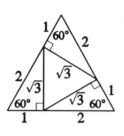

Method II: Use the law of cosines.

Problem 6-3

Method I: We must solve $x^2 + y^2 = 25$ in integers, with $x < y$. The six solutions, which arise from the identities $3^2 + 4^2 = 4^2 + 3^2 = 25 = 0^2 + 5^2 = 5^2 + 0^2$, are $\boxed{(0,5),\ (-5,0),\ (-3,4),\ (3,4),\ (-4,-3),\ (-4,3)}$.

Method II: Look for points on the graph of $x^2 + y^2 = 25$ both of whose coordinates are integers. Look only above the line $y = x$, since the problem tells us that $y > x$. The solutions are the coordinates of the highlighted points.

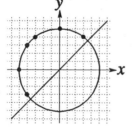

Problem 6-4

Method I: The equation $a = |a|$ is satisfied if and only if $a \geq 0$, so the original equation is true if and only if $\log_{10} x \geq 0$. Consequently, $\boxed{x \geq 1}$.

Method II: Every log graph passes through $(1,0)$. The graphs of $y = \log_{10} x$ and $y = |\log_{10} x|$ are identical when $x \geq 1$.

Problem 6-5

Take reciprocals of the terms in the first sequence to get $\frac{1}{1}, \frac{1}{2}, \frac{1}{2}, \frac{1}{3}, \frac{1}{3}, \frac{1}{3}, \frac{1}{4}, \frac{1}{4}, \frac{1}{4}, \frac{1}{4}, \ldots$. In this new sequence, the 1st term is 1. The sum of the next 2 terms is 1. The sum of the next 3 terms is 1, etc. The sum will equal 1000 when we add 1 a total of 1000 times, so $k = 1 + 2 + 3 + \ldots + 1000 = \boxed{500\,500}$.

Problem 6-6

Method I: As shown in the diagram, extend leg b of $\triangle$I until it meets altitude h drawn to b. Let the measure of the angle

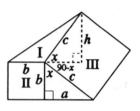

between sides b and c of the original right triangle be $x°$. Since II is a square, the extension of b makes an angle of measure $(90-x)°$ with side c of the original right triangle. Since III is a square, the angle opposite altitude h in the new right triangle has measure x. By AAS, the new triangle $\cong$ the original right triangle, so we know that $h = a$. Thus, $a^2 + b^2 = c^2$ becomes $h^2 + 19 = 95$, and $h^2 = 76$. Finally, the area of $\triangle$I $= \frac{1}{2}bh = \frac{1}{2}\sqrt{19}\sqrt{76} = \frac{1}{2}\sqrt{19}(\sqrt{19}\sqrt{4}) = \boxed{19}$.

Method II: If the measure of the angle between sides b and c of the right triangle is $x°$, then the measure of

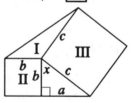

the angle between sides b and c of $\triangle$I is $(180-x)°$. The area of a triangle equals the product of the lengths of any two sides times the sine of the angle between those sides, and the sine of any angle equals the sine of its supplement; so the area of $\triangle$I $= \frac{1}{2}bc\sin(180-x)° = \frac{1}{2}bc\sin x° =$ the area of the right triangle. We know the areas of squares II and III; so $a^2 + b^2 = c^2$ becomes $a^2 + 19 = 95$, from which $a^2 = 76$. Finally, the area of $\triangle$I $=$ the area of the right triangle $= \frac{1}{2}ab = \frac{1}{2}\sqrt{19}\sqrt{76} = \frac{1}{2}\sqrt{19}(\sqrt{19}\sqrt{4}) = 19$.

Problem 1-1

Method I: Make a list of numbers which have integral square roots: $\sqrt{0} = 0$; $\sqrt{1} = 1$; $\sqrt{4} = 2$, etc. Clearly the only consecutive integers whose square roots are also consecutive integers are $\boxed{0, 1}$.

Method II: Let the two consecutive integers be x and $x + 1$. Their square roots are also consecutive integers, so $\sqrt{x} + 1 = \sqrt{x+1}$. Squaring, and subtracting $x + 1$ from both sides, we find that $x = 0$. Therefore, the integers are 0, 1.

Problem 1-2

Divide both sides by 9 to get $4 \times 5^x = 25 \times 4^y$. From this, it is clear that $(x,y) = \boxed{(2,1)}$.

Problem 1-3

We want the value of a_4, so substitute $m = 4$ into the original equation to get $\dfrac{a_4}{5} + 100 = \dfrac{1 + a_4}{4}$. Solving, $a_4 = \boxed{1995}$.

Problem 1-4

Let A be my area code. Since $A + 7$ is divisible by 7, A must be divisible by 7. Similarly, A must also be divisible by 8 and 9. The only 3-digit multiple of 7, 8, and 9 is their least common multiple, $\boxed{504}$.

Problem 1-5

The altitude from B in $\triangle RBS$ is the same as the altitude from B in $\triangle ABC$; but base $\overline{RS}$ is $\frac{1}{5}$ of base $\overline{AC}$. Therefore, the area of $\triangle RBS$ is $\frac{1}{5}$ the area of $\triangle ABC$, so the area of $\triangle RBS = \frac{1}{5}$. Similarly, the area of $\triangle QCP = \frac{1}{3}$. If c is the area of the (unshaded) intersection of $\triangle CPQ$ and $\triangle BRS$, then $a + c = \frac{1}{3}$, $b + c = \frac{1}{5}$, and $a - b = \frac{1}{3} - \frac{1}{5} = \boxed{\frac{2}{15}}$.

Problem 1-6

Let the length of the army column be 1 unit. In the diagram below, at the start, the front of the army is at the middle point, and its rear is at the left. At the end, the army column

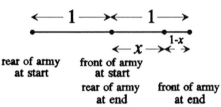

rear of army   front of army
at start   at start

rear of army   front of army
at end   at end

will have marched its own length, so its front will be at the right and its rear in the middle. Suppose the officer travels x units to reach the front of the army, where he turns around. The speeds of the officer and the army, being uniform, are proportional to their respective traveling distances in the each time period, so

$$\frac{\text{officer's speed}}{\text{army's speed}} = \frac{\text{officer's distance}}{\text{army's distance}} = \frac{1+x}{x} = \frac{x}{1-x},$$

so $x^2 = 1 - x^2$ and $x = \frac{1}{\sqrt{2}}$. Finally, the speed ratio =

$$\frac{1+x}{x} = \frac{1}{x} + 1 = \boxed{1 + \sqrt{2}}.$$

Contests written and compiled by Steven R. Conrad & Daniel Flegler   Mathematics Leagues Inc., © 1995

Problem 2-1

Every odd multiple of 5 ends in $\boxed{5}$.

Problem 2-2

By definition, $\sqrt{1+2+3+x} \geq 0$. Since $x < 10$, it follows that $0 \leq \sqrt{6+x} < 4$. The answers are the solutions to $\sqrt{6+x} = 0$, $\sqrt{6+x} = 1$, $\sqrt{6+x} = 2$, and $\sqrt{6+x} = 3$. These answers are $\boxed{-6, -5, -2, 3}$.

Problem 2-3

Method I: Divide the larger square into 4 congruent smaller squares. Rotate the larger square 90° clockwise, and it is clear that the smaller square is one-quarter of the larger square. The larger square's area is $4 \times 25 = \boxed{100}$.

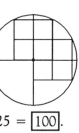

Method II: In the diagram, each dotted segment is both the hypotenuse of a right triangle and a radius of the circle; so the dotted

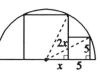

segments are congruent. In one right triangle, the legs are x and $2x$. In the other, the legs are 5 and $x+5$. By the Pythagorean Theorem, $x^2 + (2x)^2 = 5^2 + (x+5)^2$. Solving, $x = 5$; so a side of the large square is 10, and the area of the large square is 100.

Problem 2-4

At the season's end, each team, on average, has won 50% of its games; so the sum of all six winning percents is always $6(50\%) = 300\%$. The sum for the five schools whose records were known was 225%, so Hard Knox's winning record was $300\% - 225\% = \boxed{75\%}$.

Problem 2-5

Let the unknown 2-digit number be a and the unknown 3-digit number be b. Since $a\%$ of $b = 400$, it follows that $ab = 40\,000 = 2^6 \times 5^4$. Neither a nor b contains the digit 0, so neither has a factor of 10 and neither can have both 2 and 5 as factors. Thus, $a = 2^6 = 64$, $b = 5^4 = 625$, and $400 = \boxed{64\% \text{ of } 625}$.

Problem 2-6

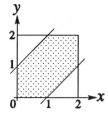

Since $0 < x < 2$ and $0 < y < 2$, we can use the coordinate plane to model the given conditions. The graph of the model is a 2×2 square in the first quadrant. Every point (x,y) inside the square meets the requirements that x and y are both positive and less than 2. The values of x and y differ by less than 1 everywhere in the shaded region, since $|x - y| < 1$ if and only if $y > x - 1$ and $y < x + 1$. The unshaded region of the 2×2 square can be reassembled to form a 1×1 square, so its area is 1. The required probability is the fractional part of the square that is shaded. This probability, which is the area of the shaded region divided by the area of the square, equals $\boxed{\frac{3}{4}}$.

Contests written and compiled by Steven R. Conrad & Daniel Flegler   Mathematics Leagues Inc., © 1995

Problem 3-1

When you subtract $1996! + 19$ from both $1996! + 19$ and $1996! + 96$, you get 0 and 77. There are as many integers between the original two numbers as there are between 0 and 77. Since we shouldn't count the endpoints, the number of such integers is $\boxed{76}$.

Problem 3-2

Let the length of a side of each square be $2x$, and let C be the point where the vertical segment through B crosses the horizontal segment through A. The lengths of the legs of right $\triangle ABC$ are $3x$ and $4x$, so $AB = 5x = 100$, and $x = 20$. Finally, the area of each square is $(2x)^2 = 40^2 = \boxed{1600}$.

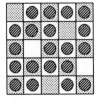

Problem 3-3

Method I: You cannot use more than 4 checkers in each row, so the number of checkers used is at most 20. The diagram shows one of several possible ways to use the maximum number of checkers, $\boxed{20}$.

[**NOTE:** In the method illustrated above, a *knight's move* enables you to move among the unoccupied squares. A *knight* is a piece in the game of chess.]

Method II: Another way to position the checkers is to put one in every small square *except* the small squares on either one of the major diagonals.

Problem 3-4

The divisors of 20 are 1, 2, 4, 5, 10, and 20; and each gives a different solution. Since $2^{20} = (2^1)^{20} = (2^2)^{10} = (2^4)^5 = (2^5)^4 = (2^{10})^2 = (2^{20})^1$, the number of solutions is $\boxed{6}$.

Problem 3-5

Method I: Since $y - x = x - 6$, $y = 2x - 6$. Substitute for y in the equation $\frac{16}{y} = \frac{y}{x}$ and simplify to get $x^2 - 10x + 9 = 0$, from which $x = 9$ or 1, and $(x,y) = \boxed{(1,-4),\ (9,12)}$.

Method II: Since $\frac{16}{y} = \frac{y}{x}$, we get $x = \frac{y^2}{16}$. Substitute into $y - x = x - 6$ to get $\frac{y^2}{16} - 6 = y - \frac{y^2}{16}$. Solving, $y = -4$ or 12, and $(x,y) = (1,-4),\ (9,12)$.

Problem 3-6

By the binomial theorem,

$$(a + bi)^4 = a^4 + 4a^3bi + 6a^2b^2i^2 + 4ab^3i^3 + b^4i^4$$
$$= a^4 + 4a^3bi - 6a^2b^2 - 4ab^3i + b^4$$
$$= (a^4 - 6a^2b^2 + b^4) + 4ab(a^2 - b^2)i$$
$$= (a^4 - 6a^2b^2 + b^4) + 4ab(a + b)(a - b)i$$
$$= \qquad c \qquad + \qquad 24i.$$

Two complex numbers are equal if and only if their real parts are equal and their imaginary parts are equal, so $4ab(a + b)(a - b)i = 24i$. Dividing both sides by $4i$, we get $ab(a + b)(a - b) = 6$, whose only solution in positive integers is $(a,b) = (2,1)$. Finally, $c = (a^4 - 6a^2b^2 + b^4) = \boxed{-7}$.

Contests written and compiled by Steven R. Conrad & Daniel Flegler   Mathematics Leagues Inc., © 1996

Problem 4-1

Method I: Pooling their resources must have left them 1¢ short of the price of a cone. Hence, Rufus must have had only 1¢, and the cost, in cents, of one cone must have been $\boxed{25 \text{ or } 25¢}$.

Method II: Let x represent the cost, in cents, of one cone. Since $x-24 + x-2 < x$, it follows that $x < 26$. Since Rufus was 24¢ short of the price of a cone, the price of a cone must have been more than 24¢. Since x is integral and $x < 26$, $x = 25$.

Problem 4-2

If the original three numbers are r, s, and t, then

$$\frac{a+b+c}{3} = \frac{\frac{r+s}{2} + \frac{r+t}{2} + \frac{s+t}{2}}{3} = \frac{r+s+t}{3} = \frac{12}{3} = \boxed{4}.$$

Problem 4-3

We are given that $\dfrac{1}{x^{1996}} = 1996^{1996}$. Take the real 1996th roots of both sides to get $\dfrac{1}{x} = \pm 1996$. Finally, take reciprocals to get $x = \boxed{\dfrac{\pm 1}{1996} \text{ or } \pm 0.0005010}$.

[**NOTE:** Since answers must be exact or must have 4 (or more) significant digits, correctly rounded, an answer of 0.0005 must **NOT** receive credit. The answer 0.0005 has only 1 significant digit, not the 4 (or more) required for an approximate answer to receive credit. Similarly, do not give credit for the answer 0.00501, since this has only 3 significant digits.]

Problem 4-4

Method I: Divide both sides of the given equation by $\cos\theta$ to get $\tan\theta = 2$. Draw the diagram at the right to see that $|\cos\theta| = \dfrac{1}{\sqrt{5}}$ and $\cos^2\theta = \boxed{\dfrac{1}{5}}$.

Method II: Square both sides of the given equation to get $\sin^2 x = 4\cos^2 x$. Add $\cos^2 x$ to both sides to get $\sin^2 x + \cos^2 x = 5\cos^2 x$, from which $\cos^2 x = \dfrac{1}{5}$.

Method III: On a TI-82 (or TI-81), with your calculator in radian mode, draw $y = \sin x$ and $y = 2\cos x$. Use **CALC** (or **ZOOM** and **TRACE**) to determine that $x = 1.1071\ldots$ is a solution, in radians, of the given equation, so $\cos^2 x = 0.2000$.

Problem 4-5

The diagram at the right shows that, when the radius of each circle is 1, the perimeter of the original equilateral triangle is $\boxed{6 + 6\sqrt{3}}$.

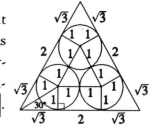

Problem 4-6

In the 50-element set $\{51, 52, \ldots, 100\}$, no number is divisible by another; so $n > 50$. Look at *any* 51-element set of integers, each ≤ 100. Each of these 51 numbers is itself odd; or, if not, it can be factored into a power of 2 times an odd number ≤ 99. Since there are only 50 odd numbers less than ≤ 99, at least two of the 51 numbers (call these two a and b) are associated with identical odd numbers (this is *the pigeonhole principle*). When the larger of a and b is divided by the smaller, the quotient is a power of 2. Hence, the least such value of n is $\boxed{51}$.

Contests written and compiled by Steven R. Conrad & Daniel Flegler   Mathematics Leagues Inc., © 1996

Problem 5-1

Method I: A quadrilateral with all sides congruent is a rhombus. The rhombus with side-length 9 that has the largest area is the square. Its area is $\boxed{81}$.

Method II: A parallelogram with sides a and b and included angle θ has area $ab\sin\theta$. The maximum area of a rhombus with side-length 9 is $81\sin 90° = 81$.

Problem 5-2

Fermat claimed (and Euler proved) that the only integer solutions to $a^3 = b^2 + 2$ are (3,5) and $\boxed{(3,-5)}$.

Problem 5-3

The statement that the numbers G and P differ by no more than 10 can be written in several ways. Most of these ways use the $\le$ symbol twice. Some examples are: $G-10 \le P \le G+10$, or $P-10 \le G \le P+10$, or $-10 \le P-G \le 10$, or $-10 \le G-P \le 10$. To use the $\le$ symbol only once, you can use any one of these:

$$|G-P| \le 10 \text{ or } |P-G| \le 10 \text{ or } (P-G)^2 \le 100 \text{ or}$$
$$(G-P)^2 \le 100 \text{ or } \sqrt{(G-P)^2} \le 10 \text{ or } \sqrt{(P-G)^2} \le 10.$$

Problem 5-4

$\log_2\left(\dfrac{x-1}{x+1}\right) > 1 \Leftrightarrow \dfrac{x-1}{x+1} > 2 \Leftrightarrow \dfrac{x-1}{x+1} - 2 > 0 \Leftrightarrow$

$\dfrac{-x-3}{x+1} > 0 \Leftrightarrow \dfrac{x+3}{x+1} < 0$. This inequality is true if and only if $x+3$ and $x-1$ have opposite signs. If $x > 1$, both are positive; and if $x < -3$, both are negative. Therefore, $\boxed{-3 < x < -1}$.

Problem 5-5

Method I: In any such series of $n > 1$ consecutive integers, $1996 = n \times$ (term average). If n is odd, the term average equals the middle term, so the term average is integral and n is a divisor of 1996. Since $1996 = 2^2 \times 499$, and 499 is prime, $n = 499$ and the term average is 4. We are not using negative numbers, so that's impossible; and n must be even. Hence, the term average is half the (necessarily odd) sum S of the two (consecutive integer) middle terms. Thus, $1996 = n \times (S/2)$, so S divides 2×1996. Since $S > 1$ is odd, $S = 499 = 249 + 250$. Continue from there with three more pairs whose sum is 499 (248 and 251, 247 and 252, and 246 and 253). The smallest number of the series is $\boxed{246}$.

Method II: The given series is $a + (a+1) + (a+2) + \ldots + (a+k) = 1996$. In any such series, the sum of the first and last terms, when multiplied by the number of terms, equals twice the sum of the series. Therefore, $(2a+k)(k+1) = 3992 = 2^3 \times 499$. Whenever $(k+1)$ is even, $(2a+k)$ is odd; and whenever $(k+1)$ is odd, $(2a+k)$ is even. To minimize a, we should maximize k. If $k+1$ is odd, then $k = 498$ or 0. The case $k = 498$ is impossible. If $k+1 = 8$, $k = 7$, $2a+k = 499$, $2a = 492$, and the least a is 246.

Problem 5-6

Checkerboarding *any* rectangle with integer sides and an area of 20 results in 10 dark and 10 light squares.

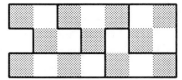

Except for the "T," each piece, when placed on *any* checkerboard, covers 2 dark and 2 light squares. The "T" covers 3 of one color and 1 of the other. The 5 pieces must cover 11 of one color and 9 of the other. This proves that *we cannot fit* all 5 pieces into an integer-sided rectangle with an area of 20. Since the 5 pieces can fit in a 3×7 rectangle in the way shown above, the least possible area is $\boxed{21}$.

Contests written and compiled by Steven R. Conrad & Daniel Flegler   Mathematics Leagues Inc., © 1996

Problem 6-1

The area of the square is $9 + 16 = 25$, so the length of a side of the square is 5, and its perimeter is $\boxed{20}$.

Problem 6-2

Since $x = y^2$, it follows that $x^{998} = (y^2)^{998} = y^{1996}$, so $y^{1996} - x^{998} + 499 = y^{1996} - y^{1996} + 499 = \boxed{499}$.

Problem 6-3

Method I: Initially, some points on the graph are $(2,8)$, $(4,4)$, ... In each case, $xy = 16$ or $y = \dfrac{16}{x}$. After applying transformation T and doubling each coordinate, these points become $(4,16)$, $(8,8)$, ... Now $xy = 64$, so $y = \dfrac{64}{x}$ and $k = \boxed{64}$.

Method II: Let $x' = 2x$ and let $y' = 2y$, so $x = \dfrac{x'}{2}$ and $y = \dfrac{y'}{2}$. Substituting into the original equation, $\dfrac{y'}{2} = \dfrac{16}{\frac{x'}{2}}$, so $y' = \dfrac{64}{x'}$.

Problem 6-4

The hypotenuse of a right triangle has the shortest altitude, so the other two altitudes <u>must be</u> the legs. The length of the hypotenuse is $\sqrt{15^2 + 20^2} = \boxed{25}$.

Problem 6-5

Method I: Add the equations to get $(x + y)^2 = 25$, from which $x + y = \pm 5$. Substitute this into each equation to get $(x,y) = \boxed{(9/5, 16/5),\ (-9/5, -16/5)}$.

Method II: This problem looks like an algebraic restatement of problem 6-1! Label the shorter dimensions of the rectangles x and y, and a side of the square is $x+y$. The given equations say that the areas of the rectangles are 9 and 16. In problem 1, we found that $x+y = 5$. Here, don't forget $x+y = -5$.

Method III: Dividing the first equation by the second, we get $x/y = 9/16$. Substituting this back into each equation, we can now find both solutions.

Method IV: Solving for $x + y$ in either equation and substituting into the other equation gives you $x/y = 9/16$ or $y/x = 16/9$. Now, proceed as in Method III.

Problem 6-6

Method I: The series $\frac{1}{2} + \frac{1}{4} + \dots + \frac{1}{2^n} + \dots$ represents the sum of the reciprocals of all the numbers whose only prime divisor is 2. The sum of this series is 1. The series $\frac{1}{3} + \frac{1}{9} + \dots + \frac{1}{3^n} + \dots$ represents the sum of the reciprocals of all the numbers whose only prime divisor is 3. The sum of this series is $\frac{1}{2}$. The product of these two series is the series whose terms are the reciprocals of all numbers divisible by *both* 2 and 3, but no other prime; its sum is $1 \times \frac{1}{2} = \frac{1}{2}$. Adding these three sums, $k = 1 + \frac{1}{2} + \frac{1}{2} = \boxed{2}$.

Contests written and compiled by Steven R. Conrad & Daniel Flegler   Mathematics Leagues Inc., © 1996

Answers &
Difficulty Ratings
November, 1991 – April, 1996

Answers

	1991-1992		**1992-1993**		**1993-1994**
1-1.	± 3	1-1.	100	1-1.	457
1-2.	1	1-2.	1	1-2.	1994
1-3.	36π	1-3.	100	1-3.	17
1-4.	3	1-4.	$\frac{1}{1992}$	1-4.	0
1-5.	$\frac{6}{5}, \frac{6}{4}, \frac{6}{3}, \frac{6}{2}, \frac{6}{1}$ or equivalents	1-5.	$\frac{1}{8}$	1-5.	3750
1-6.	$1 \le x \le 4$	1-6.	49 or \$49	1-6.	4608
2-1.	(1,9,9,1) or any rearrangement	2-1.	0	2-1.	0
2-2.	$10\sqrt{2}$ or $\sqrt{200}$	2-2.	1	2-2.	$-3, -1, 1$
2-3.	$\frac{1}{8}$	2-3.	1992	2-3.	180
2-4.	-2	2-4.	$1 < x \le 2$	2-4.	19935
2-5.	$(-1,-4), (1,4), (7,4)$	2-5.	3	2-5.	2
2-6.	3	2-6.	6	2-6.	$(0,9,1), (4,-3,9), \left(\frac{20}{9}, \frac{7}{3}, \frac{49}{9}\right)$
3-1.	2	3-1.	0	3-1.	200
3-2.	$\frac{12}{5}$	3-2.	0, 1993	3-2.	$-1, \frac{1993}{1994}$
3-3.	$1, -1, 2, -2$	3-3.	52	3-3.	936
3-4.	12	3-4.	175	3-4.	$\frac{5}{16}$
3-5.	8	3-5.	3	3-5.	$(0,0), \left(\left(\frac{7}{3}\right)^{\frac{7}{4}}, \left(\frac{7}{3}\right)^{\frac{3}{4}}\right)$
3-6.	84	3-6.	$\sqrt{\dfrac{1+\sqrt{2}}{2}}$	3-6.	$\frac{100}{249}$
4-1.	1	4-1.	$\frac{8}{25}$	4-1.	0
4-2.	24	4-2.	1992	4-2.	4
4-3.	1991, -1992	4-3.	2	4-3.	2^{3^5}
4-4.	1695	4-4.	25	4-4.	16
4-5.	2:3	4-5.	154	4-5.	-12
4-6.	$\frac{4}{\sqrt{5}}$	4-6.	$\frac{1+\sqrt{5}}{2}$	4-6.	997
5-1.	32	5-1.	B	5-1.	-1994
5-2.	3984	5-2.	8	5-2.	24
5-3.	π	5-3.	3	5-3.	45 or 45°
5-4.	32, -33	5-4.	20, 22	5-4.	$\left(\frac{1}{5}, \frac{1}{2}\right)$
5-5.	3671	5-5.	21, -21	5-5.	96, 104
5-6.	$-4 \le a \le -3$	5-6.	23	5-6.	$\frac{1}{\sqrt{15}}$
6-1.	-1	6-1.	0	6-1.	251 or \$2.51
6-2.	25	6-2.	26	6-2.	$-1, 1, 1994$
6-3.	168	6-3.	210°	6-3.	3
6-4.	67	6-4.	1994	6-4.	222
6-5.	$5, \frac{1}{5}$	6-5.	3439	6-5.	$2\sin 15°$ or $\sqrt{2-\sqrt{3}}$
6-6.	26	6-6.	$\left(\frac{1}{4}, \frac{1}{6}\right)$	6-6.	$-2 < x < 0$ or $x > 2$

Answers

1994-1995

1-1. 1994

1-2. 75

1-3. 17^2

1-4. $7\sqrt{2}$

1-5. 65

1-6. 20

2-1. ± 1

2-2. 2

2-3. Prof. Clever

2-4. 120

2-5. $\pm 4, \pm 2, 0$

2-6. 108

3-1. 20 or 20%

3-2. 16π

3-3. 120

3-4. 6

3-5. (3,3), (4,2), (5,1), (7,−1)

3-6. 98

4-1. $\sqrt{7}$

4-2. 24

4-3. (5,4) (11,8)

4-4. (−64,−64)

4-5. 27

4-6. $\frac{1995}{3978031}$ or 0.0005015

5-1. 123

5-2. 2π

5-3. 135

5-4. 0.739085133172 . . .

5-5. $\frac{1}{7}$

5-6. (8,27), (8,−27), (−8,27), (−8,−27)

6-1. 0, 1

6-2. $3\sqrt{3}$

6-3. (0,5), (−5,0), (−3,4), (3,4), (−4,−3), (−4,3)

6-4. $x \geq 1$

6-5. 500 500

6-6. 19

1995-1996

1-1. 0, 1

1-2. (2,1)

1-3. 1995

1-4. 504

1-5. $\frac{2}{15}$

1-6. $1 + \sqrt{2}$

2-1. 5

2-2. −6, −5, −2, 3

2-3. 100

2-4. 75%

2-5. 64% of 625

2-6 $\frac{3}{4}$

3-1. 76

3-2. 1600

3-3. 20

3-4. 6

3-5. (1,−4), (9,12)

3-6. −7

4-1. 25 or 25¢

4-2. 4

4-3. ± 0.0005010 or $\frac{\pm 1}{1996}$

4-4 $\frac{1}{5}$

4-5. $6 + 6\sqrt{3}$

4-6. 51

5-1. 81

5-2. (3,−5)

5-3. $|G-P| \leq 10$ or $|P-G| \leq 10$ or $(P-G)^2 \leq 100$ or $(G-P)^2 \leq 100$ or $\sqrt{(G-P)^2} \leq 10$ or $\sqrt{(P-G)^2} \leq 10$

5-4. $-3 < x < -1$

5-5. 246

5-6. 21

6-1. 20

6-2. 499

6-3. 64

6-4. 25

6-5. (9/5,16/5), (−9/5,−16/5)

6-6. 2

Difficulty Ratings

(% correct of 5 highest-scoring students from each participating school)

1991-1992		1992-1993		1993-1994		1994-1995		1995-1996	
1-1.	81%	1-1.	75%	1-1.	99%	1-1.	91%	1-1.	98%
1-2.	99%	1-2.	90%	1-2.	71%	1-2.	88%	1-2.	86%
1-3.	70%	1-3.	89%	1-3.	89%	1-3.	94%	1-3.	81%
1-4.	86%	1-4.	53%	1-4.	60%	1-4.	78%	1-4.	88%
1-5.	29%	1-5.	31%	1-5.	24%	1-5.	51%	1-5.	72%
1-6.	49%	1-6.	29%	1-6.	20%	1-6.	13%	1-6.	3%
2-1.	90%	2-1.	94%	2-1.	99%	2-1.	83%	2-1.	85%
2-2.	86%	2-2.	70%	2-2.	60%	2-2.	92%	2-2.	90%
2-3.	72%	2-3.	72%	2-3.	82%	2-3.	80%	2-3.	97%
2-4.	48%	2-4.	44%	2-4.	91%	2-4.	61%	2-4.	71%
2-5.	61%	2-5.	67%	2-5.	26%	2-5.	64%	2-5.	83%
2-6.	12%	2-6.	19%	2-6.	1½%	2-6.	13%	2-6.	22%
3-1.	97%	3-1.	98%	3-1.	92%	3-1.	92%	3-1.	80%
3-2.	78%	3-2.	81%	3-2.	85%	3-2.	77%	3-2.	70%
3-3.	70%	3-3.	80%	3-3.	87%	3-3.	78%	3-3.	78%
3-4.	83%	3-4.	63%	3-4.	16%	3-4.	59%	3-4.	52%
3-5.	6%	3-5.	58%	3-5.	19%	3-5.	20%	3-5.	54%
3-6.	1¼%	3-6.	2½%	3-6.	4%	3-6.	25%	3-6.	21%
4-1.	90%	4-1.	93%	4-1.	96%	4-1.	87%	4-1.	95%
4-2.	92%	4-2.	89%	4-2.	96%	4-2.	90%	4-2.	90%
4-3.	81%	4-3.	95%	4-3.	85%	4-3.	62%	4-3.	81%
4-4.	51%	4-4.	78%	4-4.	82%	4-4.	44%	4-4.	64%
4-5.	35%	4-5.	30%	4-5.	31%	4-5.	80%	4-5.	40%
4-6.	28%	4-6.	26%	4-6.	17%	4-6.	23%	4-6.	17%
5-1.	98%	5-1.	93%	5-1.	96%	5-1.	78%	5-1.	98%
5-2.	91%	5-2.	94%	5-2.	57%	5-2.	83%	5-2.	82%
5-3.	50%	5-3.	71%	5-3.	91%	5-3.	95%	5-3.	74%
5-4.	23%	5-4.	27%	5-4.	52%	5-4.	62%	5-4.	28%
5-5.	4%	5-5.	50%	5-5.	83%	5-5.	10%	5-5.	67%
5-6.	5%	5-6.	9%	5-6.	5%	5-6.	3%	5-6.	23%
6-1.	92%	6-1.	97%	6-1.	91%	6-1.	95%	6-1.	96%
6-2.	95%	6-2.	90%	6-2.	83%	6-2.	80%	6-2.	95%
6-3.	70%	6-3.	48%	6-3.	40%	6-3.	45%	6-3.	60%
6-4.	73%	6-4.	42%	6-4.	84%	6-4.	60%	6-4.	83%
6-5.	33%	6-5.	31%	6-5.	33%	6-5.	42%	6-5.	38%
6-6.	31%	6-6.	50%	6-6.	7%	6-6.	50%	6-6.	52%

Math League Contest Books
4th Grade Through High School Levels

Written by Steven R. Conrad and Daniel Flegler, recipients of President Reagan's 1985 Presidential Awards for Excellence in Mathematics Teaching, each book provides schools and students with problems from regional interscholastic competitions.

- Easy-to-use format designed for a 30-minute period
- Problems range from straightforward to challenging
- Contests from 4th grade through high school

1-10 copies of any one book: $12.95 each ($16.95 Canadian)
11 or more copies of any one book: $9.95 each ($12.95 Canadian)

Use the form below (or a copy) to order your books

Name _____

Address _____

City _____ State _____ Zip _____
                                   (or Province)   (or Postal Code)

Available Titles	# of Copies	Cost
Math Contests—Grades 4, 5, 6		
Volume 1: 1979-80 through 1985-86	_____	_____
Volume 2: 1986-87 through 1990-91	_____	_____
Volume 3: 1991-92 through 1995-96	_____	_____
Math Contests—Grades 7 & 8		
Volume 1: 1977-78 through 1981-82	_____	_____
Volume 2: 1982-83 through 1990-91	_____	_____
Math Contests—7, 8, & Algebra Course 1		
Volume 3: 1991-92 through 1995-96	_____	_____
Math Contests—High School		
Volume 1: 1977-78 through 1981-82	_____	_____
Volume 2: 1982-83 through 1990-91	_____	_____
Volume 3: 1991-92 through 1995-96	_____	_____
Shipping and Handling		$3.00

Please allow 4-6 weeks for delivery   Total: $_____

☐ Check or Purchase Order Enclosed; **or**

☐ Visa / MasterCard # _____

☐ Expiration Date _____ Signature _____

Mail your order with payment to:

Math League Press
P.O. Box 720
Tenafly, NJ 07670

Phone: (201) 568-6328 • Fax: (201) 816-0125